D1081335

HORNBLOWER'S NAVY

HORNBLOWER'S NAVY

LIFE AT SEA IN THE AGE OF NELSON

Steve Pope

ORION

CONTENTS

INTRODUCTION

Horatio Hornblower is the most enduring military hero in British fiction. Our apparently insatiable appetite for his adventures owes a great deal to the storytelling gifts of C.S. Forester, but also to their stirring context. As an officer in the British Royal Navy during the Napoleonic Wars, Hornblower comes to us from a uniquely romantic niche in modern history.

Gregory Peck as Captain Horatio Hornblower. Sartorial elegance aside, no Hollywood epic could outshine the true story of the Royal Navy's twenty-year struggle against France. (The Kobal Collection)

The men of Hornblower's Navy belonged in many ways to the modern world. They thought and acted in ways that are familiar to twentieth-century readers, yet they lived and worked in an age before the terror of the sea was dimmed by the blunt certainties of industrial technology. They took to the winds in fragile wooden ships, armed to the teeth against human foes but almost powerless against the elemental forces of storm and disease. In war or peace, every voyage was a dice with death, part of an unceasing struggle to tame the ocean highways.

Over the two decades of war that formed the heart of Hornblower's career, the Royal Navy defied nature to impose its writ on every corner of the globe. Studded with great battle triumphs and countless smaller victories, the Napoleonic Wars established the Royal Navy as the first truly world power, and formed an epic chapter in British martial folklore. They also provided an unparalleled fund of swashbuckling tales that have captivated generations of readers for more than sixty years.

Forester certainly knew his stuff. In the background of every Hornblower adventure, historical figures locked in a real struggle for global supremacy add an epic dimension to the storytelling. In the foreground, every naval scenario is described with loving precision, as are the lives of the men that carry them out.

Writing in the middle years of the twentieth century, Forester also brings a strong sense of the Royal Navy's proud traditions and standards to his work,

The real Hornblower? One of the Royal Navy's most audacious officers in the years after Nelson's death, James Alexander Gordon has been cited as the model for Forester's hero. (Hulton Getty)

along with genuine dash and faith in simple heroism that are hard to imitate these days.

On the other hand, there are ways in which the author's own place in time and his concern for historical accuracy clash. Constrained by contemporary etiquette and orthodoxies, he draws a discreet veil over some of the more ribald excesses of life in a service untouched by the cold hand of Victorian morality, and indulges in regular bouts of racial stereotyping. He also spares us a great deal of the fascinating, if often insanitary, detail surrounding everyday life aboard a Georgian warship, and betrays an attitude towards women in general that is at times painfully pre-feminist.

While none of these slightly warped perspectives detracts from the cut and thrust of a Hornblower yarn, the truth about the way the Georgian Navy behaved is even more interesting.

A charming mixture of reckless brilliance, introverted calculation and searing self-doubt, Hornblower himself is in many ways a superbly drawn composite of the great captains that bestrode his day. His emotional range may be a little on the narrow side, and his stiff upper lip somewhat out of place in the Enlightenment, but his talents are the real thing.

Between 1794, when Hornblower joined the Navy as a callow midshipman of seventeen, and the end of the wars with France in 1815, the service was blessed with a unique array of talent in command of its warships. Not all combined the inspiring leadership, audacious initiative and superlative seamanship of Forester's hero, but an astonishing number did.

It is no accident that Hornblower reached senior command only after the death of Nelson – no fictional hero could have surpassed the astonishing dramas of his lifetime – but the victor of the Nile, Copenhagen and Trafalgar was only the brightest star in a firmament of fighting commanders that included Pellew, Howe, Jervis, Duncan, Collingwood, Saumarez and many more. Hornblower's achievements could never be called commonplace, but they are all founded in the reality of the Royal Navy's finest hours.

So are the tens of thousands of less exalted men whose skills, endurance and dedication illuminate Forester's fiction. Confined together for months on end, the crew of a Napoleonic man-of-war formed a unique and complex community. Officers, skilled seamen, craftsmen or simple landlubbers … every man and boy fulfilled an allotted role in the life of a ship, and even the greatest commander exercised his powers only thanks to their cooperation and competence.

In conditions that are appalling by modern standards, and for scant reward, British crews faced daily peril in complete isolation from the rest of civilization. Yet the officers, men and ships of Hornblower's Navy changed the world. Backed by the wealth of industrializing Britain, they emerged from centuries of steady maritime development to claim the oceans as their own. This book tells the amazing story of how they did it.

CHAPTER ONE

HORNBLOWER'S NAVY: WONDER OF THE MODERN WORLD

A NEW WORLD POWER

The world had never seen anything like the Royal Navy that welcomed young Horatio Hornblower to a lifetime of service in 1794. On the brink of a twenty-year war that would bring unprecedented glory and lustre to its name; it was already the largest and most costly military force ever to grace the seas, and the first to achieve any kind of fighting proficiency since ships began mounting guns.

Even in peacetime, when its size and efficiency were at their lowest ebb, the Navy outclassed any potential rival. All Europe's other services were languishing in decline by the early 1790s, subordinated to the needs of almost incessant land warfare or impoverished by the constraints of crumbling feudal systems.

Britain was different. Its geographical position, an ideal springboard for oceanic adventure, had made involvement in Europe's endless frontier squabbles an avoidable option. And from its fertile admixture of climate, geography, capitalism and relative political stability had emerged the first fruits of an industrial revolution that was turning Britain into the world's workshop and warehouse.

The industrial boom made Britain's propertied classes fantastically rich. Ever-expanding merchant fleets brought a flood of cheap raw materials, cheaper commodities and import taxes into the country, and sailed away to inundate the world with manufactured goods at unbeatable prices. But as Britain got richer through the eighteenth century, it became ever more dependent on free and safe use of the seas.

Big business, Georgian style. Rowlandson's cartoon of Portsmouth Point in 1800 gives some idea of just what it took to get a great sailing navy to sea. As provisions of every kind are hauled towards the ships' boats, the port admiral's eyeglass is trained firmly on the vital link in the proceedings – the moneylender's office across the road. (By Thomas Rowlandson (1756–1827), The Bridgeman Art Library/Portsmouth City Art Gallery)

The sea lanes linking Enlightenment Europe with the wider world stretched to its farthest corners, but they were no more than a few narrow threads, still fraught with elemental dangers and easily snapped by hostile intervention. Britain's communications with a growing empire of trading posts, colonial settlements and export markets could never be fully guaranteed against storm, disease or other natural enemies, but no price was too high for a navy that could keep rivals and pirates at bay.

So while continental dynasts risked uprising, bankruptcy or both to finance their competing armies, generations of British leaders bore the cost of their incredibly expensive navy out of national profits. Like good businessmen, they invested more or less cheerfully in a sword and shield of empire that offered both security and growth.

They built and maintained warships to defend Britain's long coastlines, to expand and hold the colonies, to guard their precious seaborne cargoes and to deny their enemies access to the oceans. To make all this possible, they financed a network of bases, dockyards, personnel and bureaucracy that made the Navy the most complex industrial combine ever seen outside China.

But Britain's great, almost unwitting, experiment in the application of

OPPOSITE

Posterity has been kind to the navy of Elizabeth the First. Despite its successes, it was little more than an occasional collection of mercenary captains – and many of its enterprises ended in ignominious failure. This plan of Cadiz, made by Walter Raleigh in 1596, was the blueprint for one ill-fated attempt to repeat Drake's devastating raid of 1587. (Hulton Getty)

BELOW

An Edwardian portrayal of Alfred the Great's galleys attacking Viking longships. Alfred built England's first navy, but its impact was strictly local. In an age of simple, single-masted ships, sea power depended on the elements, and could only be exercised in the Mediterranean. (Circa 1910 by Henry A. Payne (1868–1940), The Bridgeman Art Libary/Private Collection)

sea power could not be complete as long as naval warfare remained a lottery determined by tides and winds. During the Seven Years War (1756-63) the Navy at last glimpsed the grails of operational competence and strategic coherence that had eluded every predecessor, and its triumphs signalled the full dawn of a new world order.

Thirty years on, as European armies marched into an epoch of conquest and carnage, the British could sing with certainty that Britannia ruled the waves. In an age when most people never left their home village, and when any kind of long journey was a dice with disease and death, Hornblower's Navy defied generally accepted scientific and technological limitations.

OLD WORLD POWERS

It had taken the English a very long time to translate their proximity to the sea into any kind of naval power.

While great sea battles were deciding the fates of ancient and medieval Mediterranean empires, England was not even a unified state. And as long as warships were simple, single-masted vessels, the potentates of the Ottoman empire and Venice could expect no real challenge from the storm-tossed north.

It was not until the thirteenth and fourteenth centuries that a gradual transformation in big ship design, along with improvements in navigational techniques, enabled a steady shift of naval power out of the Mediterranean.

The development of three-masted vessels, equipped with a sophisticated pattern of sails, opened the mysteries of the wider oceans to regulated human exploration, and the mantle of naval supremacy had passed to the Atlantic kingdoms of Spain and Portugal by the fifteenth century.

While the first great age of discovery was being pioneered from Cadiz and Lisbon, the English were still fully absorbed in dynastic civil wars and regular conflicts with the neighbouring Scots or French. The English kings may have owned a few ships, some of them state-of-the-art galleons, but they were too busy and too poor to challenge Iberian mastery of new worlds.

By the sixteenth century, when the English finally began to emerge into the sea lanes from a ring of

Anno 1596. den 30 Junij, sijn de Hollanders met d'Enghelsche ghecommen als Vrienden, inde Ree van Cales Males met 180 schepen, t'sanderdaechs den eersten Julij hebben sijt verradelijck inghenomen ende den 17. Julij sijnse ghedwonghen ghewest met schande t'selue te verlaten.

L'An 1596 le 30 Juing, sont les Hollandois et Anglois comme amis, entrés au Riuaige de Cales Males auecq 180 Nauires, le lendemain au premier Julet l'ot surpris par trahison, au 17 dudit ont estés contraincts de l'abandonner auecq honte.

thriving ports around their southern coasts, the world outside Europe had been given to Spain and Portugal by the Catholic church, and the period mythologized as the great age of Elizabethan sea power was more like an age of national piracy.

The navy of Drake and Hawkins may have singed the King of Spain's beard at Cadiz, and won a victory against the odds over the Spanish Armada in 1588, but it suffered many less-celebrated failures, and remained little more than a peripheral fly in Spain's imperial ointment. Furthermore it mostly consisted of privately owned ships, and was in no way a national service.

Henry VIII, the only profligate Tudor, left a fleet of some eighty royal ships, but none of his successors possessed more than about thirty at any given time. The fleets that set sail from Bristol, Plymouth and London to seek their fortunes often included royal ships, but were largely financed and owned by combines of wealthy speculators. The Crown simply functioned as a stockholder in some naval exped-itions, offering financial backing and royal commissions in return for a generous share of the profits.

The Tudor and early Stuart monarchs relied on voluntary aid for national defence, and though the English fleet that fought the war was theoretically commanded by the Lord High Admiral, a court appointee in charge of the royal ships, independent captains like Drake were in no sense members of a regulated service. There was in effect no Royal Navy.

INSTRUMENT OF EMPIRE

It was not until the country came under the control of one of its great military organizers, Oliver Cromwell, that the British Navy became an international force to be reckoned with.

The early 1650s saw greatly increased construction of government-owned warships, and the formulation of an economic policy based on foreign trade. In 1651 the first of many Navigation Acts passed through Parliament, prohibiting the import of goods to home ports except in British merchant ships. The Act and its successors were to be the keystone of British naval and imperial policy into the twentieth century, but their immediate target was the growing Dutch trade empire, and they helped trigger the first of Britain's first purely naval wars.

In the process of winning a narrow victory over the Dutch Navy, its main rival for North Sea supremacy, the British Navy (emphatically not at this stage royal) discovered its first great admiral in one of Cromwell's army officers, Robert Blake, and through him a truly coherent identity as a national fighting force.

A bureaucracy was established in the form of a Navy Board, which was to be the basis of Royal Navy administration into the nineteenth century, and formal rates of pay were laid down, along with a regular ranking system. Perhaps most significantly, as frontline experience taught him the art of naval warfare, Blake produced a set of written instructions that formalized combat tactics for the first time.

For a century after Blake's death the English steadily filled the naval power vacuum created by the manifest decline of Spain. Their empire took hold in India, grew and prospered in North America and absorbed a priceless share of the Caribbean goldmine. Their merchant fleets multiplied, and so did their Navy, flourishing as the prime instrument of imperial expansion, the steadfast guardian of trade and the guarantor of home security.

The founding father of the modern Royal Navy, Robert Blake brought the iron discipline and administrative coherence of Cromwell's armies to naval warfare. Apart from establishing North American fishing colonies – a matter of great importance to trade-conscious readers a century later – he provided the British Navy with bureaucratic and operational frameworks that were the basis for its future domination of the world's sea lanes. (Hulton Getty)

But though the Royal Navy was a major world player in the game of sea power before the mid-eighteenth century, true dominance depended on the establishment of clear fighting superiority, something no navy had ever achieved.

BROADSIDES

Early Mediterranean warships, like their Viking counterparts further north, were floating troop platforms dependent on oar power for any kind of sophisticated manoeuvre. It was hardly possible to use such vessels as weapons in themselves, and when the elements enabled opposing fleets to engage, their battles were decided by hand-to-hand slaughter.

Design improvements had made direct confrontations more likely by the Middle Ages, but the elements remained a decisive factor in many engagements, and sea battles were still soldiers' contests, fought at close quarters and usually ending after one crew boarded the other's ship.

Flaming arrows or fireships apart, warships became long-range weapons with the addition of artillery, but guns were slow even partly to replace boarding as the standard means of attack. Early naval cannon were heavy, unreliable and spectacularly inaccurate at anything other than very close range. Since wooden ships were difficult to actually sink, seaborne infantry combat remained the order of the day.

The development of lighter alloys made it possible for the bigger warships to carry dozens of guns, and by the sixteenth century the invention of gunports had enabled their centre of gravity to be lowered. A large Elizabethan man-of-war could deploy more than fifty cannon, and had become a fearsome artillery platform.

But naval orthodoxy and techniques were slow to catch up with technology. The greatest sea battle of the sixteenth century, the Battle of

OVERLEAF

Claustrophobia rules the waves! The Battle of Lepanto, fought between Habsburg Austria and the Ottoman Empire in 1571, was the most important naval engagement of the century. The last great confrontation between fleets of galleys crammed with troops, fought using time-honoured ramming and boarding tactics, it was also the swansong of Mediterranean sea power, which was about to be eclipsed by the great sailing navies of the Atlantic kingdoms. (Sixteenth century, Italian School, The Bridgeman Art Library/Museo Correr, Venice)

The Mary Rose, *a prime example of early sixteenth century warship design and a celebrated white elephant. Hugely expensive and ultimately unseaworthy, the prime function of this gigantic galleon was to promote Henry VIII's self-image as the epitome of Renaissance spelndour. (The Bridgeman Art Library/ Master and Fellows, Magdalene College, Cambridge)*

Lepanto in 1571, was fought by galleys used as transports, and the most advanced navies of the age were still committed to boarding as the most efficient means of attack.

Besides, carrying large numbers of guns could be dangerous. Wooden ships could take severe punishment from cannonballs without sinking, but could easily by destroyed by a magazine explosion, and a large man-of-war required careful handling, especially in high seas, when a single wave surging through open gunports could take it to the bottom.

Gradually, and almost by accident, the Elizabethan English became the pioneers of a new tradition in naval warfare. The Spanish and Portuguese clung to the concept of warships as adjuncts to land power, cramming relatively stately vessels with troops and generally using their guns against enemy rigging to immobilize ships prior to boarding. English warships were more mobile, more heavily armed and generally used their cannon against the body of an enemy vessel, aiming to cause maximum death and destruction before closing in for the kill.

Long before the culminating triumphs of the Seven Years War, the methods of English seamen trained in piracy and commanded by a growing class of professional officers had begun to demonstrate a marked one-on-one superiority over rivals led by conservative aristocrats. But fighting qualities meant little unless enemies could be brought to action in the first place.

As this eighteenth-century illustration testifies, superior gunnery alone could not guarantee victory in a well-matched sea fight. Riddled with cannon shot, completely dismasted and out of control, a warship could remain afloat almost indefinitely... but a single rogue spark in the powder magazine could reduce it to splinters in an instant. (Circa 1759 by Richard Paton (1717–91), The Bridgeman Art Library/Bonhams, London)

The best navies of the age used their big guns as close-range weapons, holding their fire until the last possible moment before delivering a massed broadside. The effect of twenty or more cannon into the body of a wooden ship from perhaps fifty yards is well illustrated by this clash of October 1812 between the American frigate United States *and the British* Macedonian. *(By Thomas Birch (1779–1851), The Bridgeman Art Library/Historical Society of Pennsylvania, USA)*

Even in the seventeenth century, standards of seamanship and service coherence were so generally poor that naval warfare largely consisted of missed opportunities and shipwrecks. On the rare occasions when both sides could be mustered for a major battle, and ships' captains could be persuaded to risk aggression, they fought chaotic and usually inconclusive engagements. By the early eighteenth century, most navies regarded actually fighting battles as a waste of time, lives and, above all, money.

Only the British felt differently. The Royal Navy's steady growth in size and status was accompanied by an accumulating interest in technical excellence, and by increasing confidence in its own fighting ability. Seeking to assert this perceived superiority, the British looked for aggressive roles in wartime, trying to engineer confrontations with rival fleets and imposing more or less effective blockades on hostile coastlines.

Once their technical progress had enabled the British to get large numbers of ships where they wanted them, when they wanted them, the Royal Navy was in position to demonstrate the true potential of sea power.

DANGEROUS GAME

The same steady learning process that brought the Royal Navy its fighting superiority gave it one other vital advantage over rivals – relative good health.

All through the two centuries separating Drake from Hornblower, naval enterprise was haunted by the grim reaper. Storms and navigational hazards took an enormous toll of long-range shipping, but disease was the greatest threat to the lives of seamen throughout, and the British maintained the cleanest, best fed crews afloat. Though the lives of Royal Navy officers and men could be brutish and short by modern standards, they were generally longer and less unpleasant than those of their foreign counterparts, so that the British usually fought their naval campaigns with fitter, happier crews than their enemies.

Even so, nobody setting out on a long tropical voyage could confidently expect to survive. Commissioned officers might risk all for the chance of wealth or glory, but the manifest willingness of lower ranks to face the perils of service at the ends of the earth tells us something about the life they were leaving. The Georgian Navy was a dangerous and uncomfort-

The admiral's barge, almost dwarfed by his flag, returns to Plymouth after visiting two ships-of-the-line moored in the bay. As long as he was in home waters, an eighteenth-century naval commander could expect regular communication with his Admiralty masters, but an admiral at sea or on an overseas station was beyond effective government control. (By Dominic Serres (1722–93), The Bridgeman Art Library/Park Walk Gallery, London)

able home, but Georgian Britain could be worse.

If the men that served the imperial Royal Navy were motivated by bravery, greed and optimism, so were the governments that employed them. Even if long-range naval expeditions survived storm, disease, very imprecise navigational systems and dangerously unreliable charts, central control over their operations disappeared with their sails over the horizon.

Intercontinental voyages could take months, and even news transmitted between London and the Mediterranean could arrive several weeks out of date. Central authorities had no choice but to rely completely on the competence and discretion of field officers, and it was much easier to reach admiral's rank in the Georgian Navy than to become an active over-seas commander, an honour generally reserved for those blessed with outstanding skill or luck.

The best field commanders could be thoroughly out of tune with European priorities by the time they reached their stations, and their achievements were often meaningless or counterproductive in a strategic context. Unable to either influence or confirm results, governments could only hope for the best, and learn to treat even that with caution.

Though the return of a commerce raiding fleet with a train of merchant prizes was an undisputed success, the triumphs of empire building were less certain. Many a victorious colonial squadron came home to find that diplomatic shifts had made enemies allies, and that its conquests had already been given back.

Nelson with the inshore squadron off Cadiz in 1797. This type of 'close blockade', with frigates stationed constantly at the mouth of a hostile harbour, was the only genuinely effective means of strangling enemy commerce, but took a heavy toll on ships and crews required to stay on patrol for months at a time. (By Thomas Buttersworth (1768–1842), The Bridgeman Art Library/Christie's Images)

WORLD SERVICE

Far-flung colonial expansion was just one of many roles assigned to the Royal Navy at the start of the wars with France. No other army or navy in the world was burdened with responsibilities on a comparable scale, and they were enough to stretch even British imperial resources.

Merely patrolling Britain's global empire was an enormous job, involving the permanent maintenance of powerful forces in the Caribbean and the Mediterranean, as well as smaller squadrons in the Indian Ocean, Canada and off South America. Additional forces were needed in wartime to spearhead the acquisition of new colonies and defend the Empire against predators, be they hostile European fleets, privateers or local pirates. Commerce in transit needed protection against the same threats, and the Navy was also required to assign warships as escorts for convoys wherever the danger was greatest.

In European terms, the Navy was expected to blockade enemy coasts, preventing hostile warships or merchant cargoes from entering or leaving ports, and prohibiting any neutral trade in war materials. In 1793 this called for the deployment of a large fleet cruising off the west coast of France, and the strengthening of Mediterranean forces to pen French warships inside Toulon, but war with Spain and the Netherlands soon multiplied the commitment involved, and later entanglements in Baltic warfare would extend it still further.

Island Britain also looked to the Navy for national defence, and kept powerful fleets in home waters at all times. Ships at Plymouth guarded the vital southwestern approaches; fleet units at Portsmouth, Spithead and Dover held the Channel frontier with France, and the North Sea was overseen from the Nore, Lowestoft and Yarmouth … but these were just the major bases along an English coastline that enjoyed the heaviest naval protection in the world.

All this did not mean that the Navy was spared commitment in the old-fashioned way, as an adjunct to land warfare. Apart from providing transport and offshore support for military operations overseas, British

Nelson's fleet moves in to attack the French battle line at the Nile. Royal Navy commanders were expected to attack hostile forces whenever the chance arose, and despite the range of its other responsibilities, the service regarded destruction of enemy fleets as its prime function – a view not shared by the French Navy or any other rival. (National Maritime Museum)

warships were expected to operate as floating coastal fortresses, using their guns and crews to mount independent attacks against towns or military installations.

Last but by no means least, the Royal Navy was the only maritime force afloat that actively sought combat. From the smallest gunship to the mightiest fleet, British naval units went to sea under instructions to fight the enemy wherever and whenever possible, on pain of court-martial. The fate of Admiral Byng, shot in 1757 for failing to attack Spanish forces at Minorca with sufficient vigour, was untypically harsh, but Voltaire was right in thinking it encouraged the others.

Of course, no one but the British could afford to risk the loss of major warships on a regular basis. A navy was an expensive item to maintain, much more so than any contemporary army, and the wartime cost of building, manning and running the Royal Navy dented even the fabled wealth of Albion.

Constructed using specialist, often imported raw materials, a big warship could cost £100,000 to build in an age when £200 a year made a man wealthy. By 1793 the British possessed 175 big ships-of-the-line, some of them several decades old but most at least potentially serviceable,

Spearhead of Empire. Admiral Jervis bombards Fort Royal, capital of French Martinique, prior to its capture by British troops in 1794. The Navy was a highly effective weapon of imperial expansion throughout the Napoleonic Wars, but the need to send squadrons all over the world diluted its strategic impact in Europe. (Hulton Getty)

The launch of HMS Trafalgar *at Chatham in 1820. These towering battleships were among the great technological achievements of the pre-industrial age, and Britain was the only nation rich enough to produce them in large numbers. (John Whichelo (d. 1865), The Bridgeman Art Library/Christie's Images)*

along with several hundred smaller vessels.

Each time a warship went to sea, it needed sufficient supplies of water, biscuit, ammunition, gunpowder, hemp, sailsheets, spare timber, livestock, preserved food, beer, rum and many other vital commodities for anything up to 900 men on a journey that might last months, and had to be replenished at regular intervals on overseas stations. The Navy also spent big money on the construction, supply and maintenance of bases, on pay for about 100,000 seamen by 1795, and on the management of recruitment, internal affairs and supply.

All told, Britain spent an average of £30 million pounds per annum on the Navy during the twenty-two years of war after 1793. Though this amounted to only some 15% of the British government's annual expenditure by 1814, the Prussian government only spent a total of some £6 million each year, and even the world's second biggest economic power, France, recorded an annual government outlay of less than £50 million throughout the war period.

Under the circumstances, it is hardly surprising that the British as a people regarded their Navy as something special. Eighteenth-century parliaments accepted enormous naval budgets without serious protest, and pride in the Navy's achievements manifested itself at every level of British society.

In a nation that mistrusted standing armies, soldiers were generally viewed (with some justification) as what Wellington later called the 'scum of the earth'. But a British sailor ashore could expect respect from his countrymen, and a commissioned naval officer was a figure of genuine social standing, regardless of wealth or background.

By the later decades of the century the Navy was popularly regarded as invincible. 'Rule Britannia' had become the Empire's unofficial national anthem, and the Navy the most potent symbol of its prosperity. Not quite everybody loved a sailor or his employers – civil authorities in coastal regions fought a ceaseless war of jurisdiction with their naval counterparts, and the service was the scourge of merchant skippers competing for precious crews – but the Navy was generally seen as responsible for the warm sense of security and opportunity that characterized eighteenth-century Britain.

STATE OF THE NAVIES

The Navy of the Seven Years War had won victory without tears. The Empire had been enlarged and secured, European rivals had been dispatched, but the war's impact on British home life hardly extended beyond the astonishingly regular celebration of decisive victories in faraway places. Despite the loss of the United States to independence, a failure generally blamed on the Army, Britannia's confidence in her naval supremacy, and in the breed of men that exercised it, had become ingrained to the point of complacency by the 1790s.

The port at Brest. The ring of naval bases that protected southern England prevented any other sea power from disputing control of the Channel, but the French Navy's strongest fleet was at Brest, poised to exploit any lapse in the Royal Navy's defensive vigilance. (By Jean-François Hue (1751–1823), The Bridgeman Art Library/Musée de la Marine, Paris)

Though it was still far and away the world's most powerful, a period of relative neglect by mercantile, pacifist governments had left the Navy in a depressed state. Wooden ships too long in dock had begun to rot, a skeleton roster of some 10,000 personnel could barely handle the few fleet units ready for service, and peacetime conditions had allowed commands to remain in the hands of elderly men, long on tradition but short of vigour.

It took almost five years of war for the Royal Navy to shake the kinks out of its system, and for a new generation of fighting admirals to re-establish Britain's grip on the world's oceans. Meanwhile the service struggled to meet its far-flung commitments with insufficient resources, giving rivals one last chance to mount a serious challenge to the British Empire's control of the seas.

From time to time during the eighteenth century, the French Navy had seemed on the point of presenting a genuine threat to British domination. Its warships were the fastest and most manoeuvrable in the world, if none too sturdy, and its largely noble officer corps had produced a steady stream of enterprising commanders, but it had virtually given up the ghost by 1793. It had suffered from lack of funds as its royal political masters staggered from bankruptcy to oblivion, and was burdened with essentially defensive fighting tactics, but the social upheavals of the French Revolution had caused the most serious damage.

Almost every senior French naval officer fled abroad in the years after 1789, and inexperienced wartime commanders found themselves operating with unskilled but politically volatile crews under the eyes of government commissars. Though French fleets could occasionally get past British blockades without suffering shipwreck or mutiny, they were never given priority over a rapidly expanding national army, and were always denied the manpower, supplies and raw materials basic to any kind of aggressive strategy.

The proud Spanish Navy was still large, but most of its ponderous warships were little more than rotting hulks, trapped in dock because the government was permanently penniless. Though Spanish naval officers were heirs to a long and glorious naval tradition, their technical abilities were not matched by an appreciation of modern tactical priorities. Their crews, drawn from the dregs of Spanish society, were ill-fed, hardly ever paid and housed in appallingly insanitary conditions. Even when Spanish warships were able to limp to sea in numbers, they could not expect to operate efficiently or safely for very long.

Although the emerging empire of Russia was rapidly becoming a naval power in the Black and Baltic Seas, the Dutch Navy was the only other naval force with global pretensions, but it too had been denied funds during the later eighteenth century. Though it remained the only service to rival the Royal Navy in terms of efficiency, morale and good health, it had been allowed to decline by a penny-pinching ruling elite, and was simply too small to present any real threat to British dominion. Otherwise Europe's navies were either virtually useless (like the crumbling Ottoman, Venetian, Portuguese or Neapolitan fleets) or were designed purely for local operations, like the fairly powerful but largely specialist fleets belonging to the Scandinavian kingdoms.

This was the naval world in which Hornblower began his extraordinary career. It was a world apart from the progress of affairs on land, and a world in which the Royal Navy was the dominant, uniquely powerful element. It was also a world at war, in which Hornblower and his kind would be asked first to prove, and then to defend, their right to shape the next hundred years of human history.

CHAPTER TWO

HEARTS OF OAK: FIGHTING SHIPS & WEAPONS

Horatio Hornblower inhabited a world without railways, automobiles or powered flight. Sailing ships were the fastest and most reliable mode of long-distance travel or heavy haulage, as well as the only means of getting out of Britain. Even journeys that could be made using horse-drawn overland vehicles were often quicker and safer using coastal or river vessels, despite the appearance of the first tarmac roads and inland canals.

It was an age more accustomed than our own to dealing with death on an individual basis, but it was spared our weapons of mass destruction. Without machine-guns, tanks or guided missiles, it fought its battles with muskets, sabres, brute force and artillery. In this world the cannon was king, and until the twentieth century there was only one way to move powerful artillery around with any kind of efficiency – aboard ships.

Even the smallest cannon-armed vessel constituted a highly mobile, if fragile, coastal strike force, and by the 1790s a single warship could carry more than a hundred heavy guns, along with enough ammunition for several days' reasonably sustained combat. Unless opposed by a comparable ship, a big man-of-war could dominate a long stretch of coastline, and almost destroy any unfortified town within navigable range.

Deployed in numbers, these floating fortresses could deliver massive artillery attacks against hostile shipping or coastal targets almost anywhere on earth, and navies had long since learned to group warships of every size in combinations designed for particular tasks.

FLEETS, SQUADRONS AND FLOTILLAS

At the top of the operational scale, a battle fleet was the superweapon of its day. Built around a large number of the heaviest warships operating as a unit, a Royal Navy fleet was expected to dominate both its designated theatre of operations and the surrounding coasts. By convention, Royal Navy fleets included at least ten big ships, but the upper limit was determined only by availability and the practicalities of large-scale manoeuvre in a particular seaway. Smaller, faster warships generally sailed with a fleet to perform reconnaissance or communications duties, and circumstances might also dictate the presence of slower specialist warships or troop transports.

Sloops and other light craft in action on Lake Erie in 1813. This famous battle between British and American light forces was one among dozens of miniature fleet actions fought by Royal Navy squadrons all over the world during the Napoleonic Wars. The British were almost always victorious on these occasions, which is why the US Navy's comprehensive success on Lake Erie was such a massive boost to its self-esteem. (Hulton Getty)

A fleet was usually commanded by a vice-admiral, but deaths at sea or the division of large fleets in the field frequently gave command to rear-admirals, or to captains in the temporary rank of commodore. Similar flexibility attended the command of smaller groups, known as squadrons and often led by commodores, who could be picked for talent rather than seniority. Small squadrons that included no big ships were distinguished as flotillas.

A squadron might be a battle fleet in miniature, built around a few big ships and deployed to dominate a relatively small area, but any number of other warship combinations could be and were sent out with particular duties in mind. The kind of force needed for an assault on a coastal fortress, bulging with troops and heavy guns, was very different from that best suited to commerce protection duties, when the principal enemies were fast privateers or light warships.

As the Navy's roles had multiplied over the decades, careful selection of horses for courses went hand in hand with the classification of warships into distinct fighting categories, each with one or more specific roles in the broad tableau of naval warfare.

MEN-OF-WAR

Contemporary warships fell into distinct classes. Ships-of-the-line were the largest warships afloat, ranging in size from old 50- or 64-gun vessels, through the most common 74- and 80-gun ships, to massive, three-decked floating castles carrying between 100 and 130 guns. They were used in fleets or smaller groups to fight each other, to escort and support land forces overseas, and as the mainstays of blockades, but also functioned as powerful individual weapons against commercial traffic or coastal targets.

The development of frigates (26 to 44 guns) for operations alongside ships-of-the-line had followed from one of the most basic problems facing navies at sea: in an age before telegraph or radio, let alone radar or powered flight, finding a target (or even a landfall) could be a slow and fruitless process. The eyes of battle fleets on patrol or blockade duty, and powerful detached weapons in their own right, fast frigates also performed as 'cruisers', policing coastlines and sea lanes as part of a constant campaign fought by all wartime navies for control of global trade routes.

The bulk of this background war was conducted by light naval forces, with three-masted sloops or corvettes (purpose-built, single-decked warships of 10–24 guns) often the most powerful vessels operating in their sectors. The British built hundreds of sloops in wartime, the other major navies at least dozens, and they were frequently the flagships of minor forces like the token Austrian and Prussian Navies.

These were not precise definitions. What constituted a sloop, or indeed a ship fit to join a battle line, was essentially a matter of opinion. To provide itself with a more precise operational guide, the Royal Navy also categorized – or 'rated' – its larger warships according to gun count. A vessel mounting more than 90 cannon was designated a first-rate warship, second-rates

carried 80-90 guns and third rates 64 or more. Anything down to 44 guns was a fourth-rate, fifth-raters begun at 30 guns, and the smallest-rated warships were in the sixth class, armed with at least 20 guns.

Lower down the scale, light forces and minor navies could include a bewildering variety of smaller or converted ships, including cutters, brigs, gunboats, galleys and armed merchantmen, all engaged in operations against enemy light forces, merchant traffic, pirates or privateers.

SHIPS-OF-THE-LINE

The biggest warships were known as 'ships-of-the-line' or 'line of battle ships'. These were the vessels deemed large and powerful enough to sail in a 'line of battle', the formation generally adopted by fleets going into concerted action, and it was well into the nineteenth century before the abbreviation 'battleship' became commonplace.

Ships-of-the-line were primarily designed to fight each other in fleets, smashing away with their powerful broadsides until opponents sank or surrendered. They also operated in smaller squadrons or on their own, but relative lack of speed meant that fleets were almost always accompanied by smaller vessels acting as their eyes and ears. Without these, ships-of-the-line could still escort even slower troopships or convoys, and operate around static coastal positions, but they couldn't expect to track down an enemy in the open sea.

Though undoubtedly formidable weapons, ships-of-the-line were both clumsy and fragile. Manoeuvrable only by experts, they could be virtually paralysed for weeks at a time by contrary winds, and needed the luck of a fair wind to close within striking range of even a static target. Deep-keeled and relatively sluggish, they were always at risk from storms or inshore shallows, and carried more than enough gunpowder to blow them to bits in the event of fire.

More ships-of-the-line were wrecked, run aground or accidentally burned during the 1792–1815 period than were knocked out by any kind of hostile action. Each loss constituted something of a national disaster, and though some Royal Navy battleships captains were guilty of exaggerated caution, all were acutely aware that they controlled a hugely expensive symbol of national prestige.

The addition of copper bottoms to hulls, greatly reducing wear and tear, was the most important advance in shipbuilding techniques during the eighteenth century, and construction of a ship-of-the-line still stretched pre-industrial craftsmanship to the limit. Only the largest and best-equipped dockyards could build them, and their efforts were often far from flawless. Many active vessels laboured under mysterious design faults, like the unexplained imbalance that forced HMS *Victory*, perhaps the most famous fighting ship of the age, to sail with an extra 38 tons of corrective ballast permanently in its holds.

The largest ships-of-the-line were towering castles with three gun decks, mounting between 90 and 130 cannon. They weighed around 2,000 tons, and went to sea with a full complement of between 750 and 900 men, but another 50 might be crammed inside when a commanding admiral hoisted his flag on board.6

Particularly favoured by the Spanish and French Navies, but also used as flagships by the Royal Navy, these monsters could produce a devastating broadside, but were cumbersome battle weapons and seldom able to punch their weight in action.

The major European navies based their battle lines on more handy 80- or 74-gun two-deckers. About 50–55 metres long, they weighed almost as much as the three-deckers, but could be crewed by as few as 600 men. Every navy also included smaller, older two-deckers in its battle lines. Vessels mounting 60–70 guns (usually 64) were not uncommon, and old 50-gunners were still operating with British fleets in the 1790s, the smallest of them employing about 300 men.

Though by no means built on standard lines, ships-of-the-line more than any other class reflected the different priorities motivating

A fearsome sight in full flow, but a clumsy weapon of war. The giant three-deck battleships favoured by the French and Spanish Navies were generally used as flagships, but seldom punched their weight in battle. This was the French Montagne *in 1794, when it was Admiral Villaret's flagship at the Battle of the First of June. (By Philip James de Loutherbourg (1740–1812), The Bridgeman Art Library/Victoria & Albert Museum, London)*

HMS VICTORY

The most celebrated warship of the age and Nelson's flagship at Trafalgar, HMS *Victory* was launched at Chatham in 1765. A typical three-decker, built to accommodate the extra personnel that accompanied an admiral at sea, its forty-year active career was about average for a contemporary British ship-of-the-line. The design fault that forced the ship to sail with 38 tons of corrective ballast was equally unexceptional, and had no discernible ill-effect on its fighting performance, or on the durability that enabled it to survive terrible punishment during Nelson's last battle. (Colin Mudie, Weidenfeld & Nicolson Archive)

Sixteenth century shipwrights at work using techniques that, with minor refinements, would be used to build massive eighteenth century battleships like the Victory. *(The Bridgeman Art Library/ Master and Fellows, Magdalene College, Cambridge)*

the main European navies. The French built the fastest and most manoeuvrable big warships, in line with their interests in avoiding big battles and raiding British commerce lanes. British designs were altogether less handy, but generally more durable, as befitted ships likely to be on active duty for much of the time.

Other nations tended to imitate one or the other style, except for the Dutch, whose shallow home waters had given rise to a beamier, flatter-bottomed design, that tended to be clumsy in anything but perfect weather conditions.

Ships-of-the-line were generally regarded as an index of naval power, and it almost goes without saying that the Royal Navy, which deployed several large fleets simultaneously, owned more than anybody else.

At the start of the wars in 1793, the British could call on about 175 big ships, most of them in reasonably good condition. Though about half were in dock ('ordinary' in naval parlance), few had decayed beyond service. The next biggest navy, the French, possessed only 81 line of battle ships, but at least half of them were unseaworthy, and most of the Spanish Navy's 74 big fleet units had rotted away to near uselessness during long spells idle in dock.

Russia seemed able to keep a reasonably large number of its 67 ships-of-the-line at sea in time of war, but their poor condition was often a severe operational drawback, and only the relatively insignificant northern European fleets of the Netherlands (44 ships-of-the-line), Denmark (38) and Sweden (27) could claim that their major units were kept generally ship-shape most of the time.

During the two decades of war that followed, the Royal Navy slowly increased its overall strength, and was able to retire many of its older battleships as new vessels were built or captured. Meanwhile every other European navy, the Russians apart, suffered serious wartime decline, and by 1815 their few surviving ships-of-the-line had long ceased to represent any serious threat to British supremacy.

FRIGATES

Nelson once wrote that, after his death, the words 'want of frigates' would be found engraved on his heart. Other admirals might have put it less flamboyantly, but they all wanted frigates.

Smaller and faster than ships-of-the-line, frigates generally mounted between 28 and 44 guns on two decks, weighed anything from 500 to 850 tons, and carried 200–300 crewmen. Originally developed as the 'eyes' of a battle fleet on manoeuvres, they could also operate as 'cruisers', patrolling trade routes, watching blockaded harbours, or functioning as

Greyhound of war. The Royal Navy's 38-gun Galatea *shows off the sleek, clean lines of a frigate as the wind fills its sails off the Isle of Wight. (By Thomas Whitcombe (1760–1824), The Bridgeman Art Library/Bonhams, London)*

long-range commerce raiders.

Liable to be pulverized if attacked by a ship-of-the-line, but usually quick enough to escape the danger, frigates sailed with battle fleets, and were often the principal vessels in smaller squadrons, but were also the most secure and efficient class of warship for solo operations. In short, they were the most consistently useful warships afloat, and the Royal

Navy could never get enough of them.

Speed, power and relative comfort also made frigates the carriers of choice for important cargoes in a hurry, and they often functioned as long-distance transport for VIPs. Napoleon Bonaparte requisitioned a frigate to rush him from Egypt to France and supreme power in 1799, and more than fifteen years later he completed his final journey into tropical exile aboard a British frigate.

Frigates tended to get involved in a lot more fighting than bigger ships. A confrontation between battle fleets was a rarity, and often ended indecisively, but wartime actions between individual or small groups of frigates took place somewhere in the world on an almost weekly basis. Though these were sometimes inconclusive, frigate commanders on all sides tended to be the boldest of their breed, and the wars were littered with miniature epics of tenacity and good seamanship.

They usually ended in a British victory, and the Royal Navy's frigate captains were its popular heroes during the first years of war, when enticing enemy fleets into big battles was proving difficult. Chief among these paragons of derring-do was the Cornishman, Edward Pellew, whose many successes in the 1790s included the Navy's first combat victory of

After surrendering to Royal Navy forces at Rochefort in 1815, Napoleon strikes a famously grumpy pose aboard the 64-gun British ship-of-the-line Bellerophon. *He was subsequently transferred to a faster frigate for the long journey into lifetime exile on St Helena. (Hulton Getty)*

the wars, and a spectacular rampage through a confused French fleet heading for Ireland late in 1796.

It was against a member of that fleet on its return journey, in January 1797, that Pellew performed the one military feat considered beyond even the most audaciously handled frigate, when his *Indefatigable*, aided by the frigate *Amazon*, hounded a 74-gun French ship-of-the-line to destruction.

On 13 January, 1797, Captain Pellew's frigate Indefatigable *sighted the French 74-gun* Droits de l'Homme *in a gale off Brest. High seas rendered the battleship's lower guns useless as Pellew, joined by the frigate* Amazon, *chased it downwind. The* Droits de l'Homme *was eventually wrecked on the rocks, killing hundreds. The* Amazon *was also wrecked, but most of its crew survived. (By Thomas Luny (1759–1837), The Bridgeman Art Library/Falmouth Art Gallery, Cornwall)*

The Royal Navy could call on about 150 frigates for service in 1793, and numbers rose steadily to peak at more than 220 by the early nineteenth century. This still left British admirals begging for more, but they were rich beyond the dreams of their enemies.

France lost half its 69 frigates to accident or action in the first ten years of the war, and survivors hardly dared put to sea thereafter. The Dutch Navy, which owned 43 good frigates in the early 1790s, had effectively been broken up by 1800, and its remnants then rotted in harbour. A similar fate eventually befell twenty Danish Navy frigates and the few seaworthy examples left to Spain, which had owned about fifty in the early 1790s.

The only other militarily significant forces in Europe, Russia and

Sweden, began the wars with 36 and twelve frigates respectively, and built a few more in wartime, but were strictly local in outlook, and were anyway British allies for most of the time. By 1815 there was only one navy in the world with frigates that could outfight the Royal Navy, and it hadn't even existed in 1793.

Frigates were easier to build than ships-of-the-line, and gave good all-round value for money. So when prudent traders of an infant United States decided it needed a navy in 1794, they built a few large, strong frigates and sent them to mind their merchant traffic.

By the time war broke out with Britain in 1812, the new US Navy had already served notice of its talents in minor wars against the French in the West Indies, and against the Barbary pirates menacing its Mediterranean traders. Triggered by the Royal Navy's globally unpopular policy of seizing neutral vessels suspected of trading with the enemy, the Anglo-American War was little more than a series of desultory skirmishes on land. At sea it was a disaster for American overseas trade, as the Royal Navy imposed the kind of tight blockade that had started the trouble in the first place, but brilliantly handled US Navy frigates won a succession of minor but resounding victories in single-ship actions.

Oliver Hazard Perry – the US Navy's first hero and father to a great tradition of naval enterprise – commanding light forces against the British on Lake Erie in 1813. After a highly successful career as commodore of the Great Lakes flotilla, Perry moved south to the Potomac for the last months of the Anglo-American War. He died of yellow fever in 1819 while on a mission to aid anti-Spanish rebels in South America. (Hulton Getty)

These were the only defeats suffered by major units of the wartime Royal Navy that could be put down to superior technical skill or morale, and they pointed the way to a distant age of American sea power.

SLOOPS

Specialist vessels apart, sloops were the lightest class of purpose-built warship, though many smaller craft served as converted men-of-war. Sloops were flush-decked ships with a single line of guns for a broadside, but beyond that the term was something of a naval catch-all, applied to almost any warship with three masts (anything with fewer was considered a boat).

Not intended for work with battle fleets, sloops were often the most powerful warships in their sphere of operations. In this scene from the Anglo-American War of 1812, the US Navy sloop Wasp *(on the right) is making its superiority count against the British brig* Frolic. *(By Richard Willis (living artist), The Bridgeman Art Library/Private Collection)*

Sloops could be armed with as few as eight or as many as 24 guns, and could weigh anything between 100 and more than 500 tons. Though they merited the command of a full captain, their complements seldom rose above about 150 men, and could be half that.

To add to the general confusion, common parlance expanded the class far beyond even the vague Royal Navy definitions, including men of war rigged with two masts, as brigs or ketches, and single-masted cutters known as 'West India' sloops. The corvette, originally a French design, was essentially indistinguishable from a sloop, and the terms had become interchangeable by the end of the wars.

Often the largest ships in service with minor navies, sloops seldom operated with Royal Navy battle fleets, except as courier vessels or long-range scouts, but they were mainstays of the struggle for control of trade routes that played as a rolling backdrop to global warfare. Although they could seldom catch stripped-down privateers in a straight race, the best sloops were fast enough to outrun any larger warship, strong enough to survive rough seas and powerful enough to overcome most coastal raiders.

The Royal Navy started the wars with only about 120 sloops, fewer than a French Navy which regarded commerce warfare as its prime function. The French and other navies kept their light forces in action long after their fleet units had been allowed to decay, but their strength still dwindled steadily in wartime. The British meanwhile commissioned hundreds of new sloops, testimony to their value as relatively inexpensive guardians of the commercial Empire.

OPPOSITE

This unofficial graphic includes a wealth of detail, but not all of it is entirely acurate, and it conveys only a superficial impression of the mighty Royal Navy in 1804. The splendid battleships and model officers given prominence were the public face of sea power, but much of the Navy's most important work after 1805 devolved on the less imposing sloops and specialist craft needed for coastal or patrol operations. (National Maritime Museum)

LIGHT FORCES

Armour was not a factor in contemporary naval warfare. Most British warships smaller than sloops, including hundreds of yachts, cutters and other basically civilian craft, were militarized by simply adding guns and naval personnel, but small specialist warships were more carefully adapted to carry out particular operations.

Special-purpose vessels in regular Royal Navy use included gunboats, 'bombs', fireships and floating batteries, although the latter were simply armed hulks, towed into position to provide static bombardment. Other navies took the lead in designing specialist shallow-draught vessels. The French produced hundreds of armed barges for their planned invasions of England, though they were never put to serious test, and the Baltic powers operated fleets of flat-bottomed gunships designed specifically for use in its treacherously shallow channels.

BOMBS

Named after the missiles they brought to bear, naval bombs were shallow-draught vessels, strengthened to carry one or (more usually) two heavy mortars and withstand their recoil. Bombs were usually employed as mobile siege artillery, supporting a fleet or squadron against coastal fortifications.

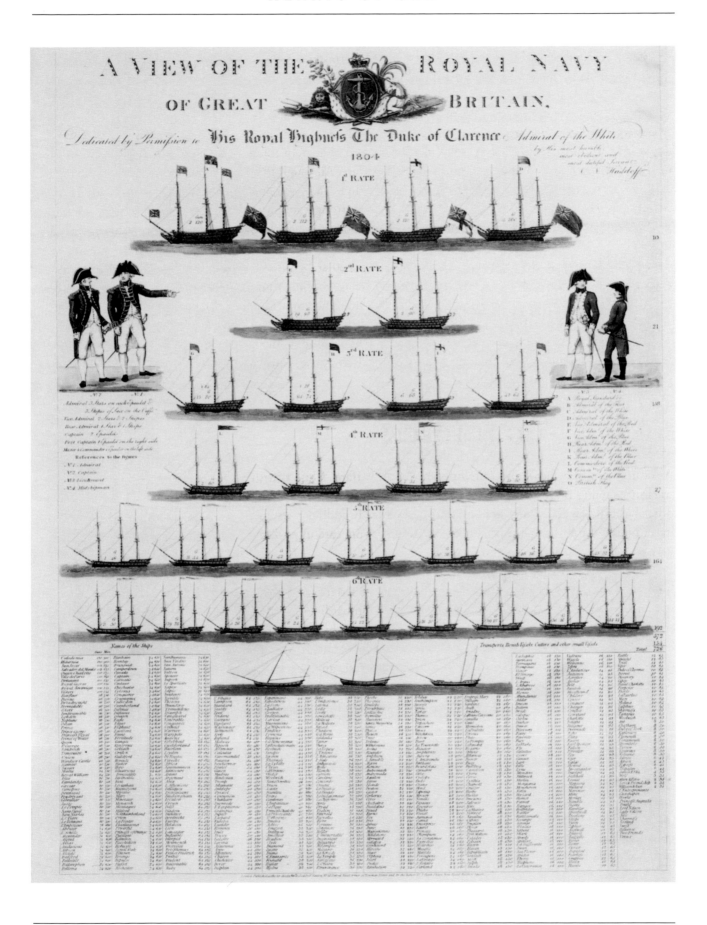

The Royal Navy made less regular use of 'bomb-ships', which were hulks packed with gunpowder and exploded near a target. Extremely vulnerable to hostile fire, they could only be used when an enemy was effectively blind, as at the Basque Roads in 1809.

FIRESHIPS

One of best-known naval tactics, and beloved of British naval romance since the Armada, the use of old ships set aflame to spread fire and confusion among hostile fleets was rare by the late eighteenth century.

Because all warships were wooden, and fireships could not be navigated during their final approaches, a change of wind could prove disastrous for the attacking side, and fleet commanders never risked deliberately letting fire loose amid the crowded chaos of a close-quarters battle.

Fireships were only really an option against enemy ships in harbour, and were even then something of a last resort. Usually employed in their allotted role only if strong coastal artillery made any other approach impossible, fireships spent most of their careers functioning as small sloops, mounting 8–10 guns.

GUNBOATS

Contemporary gunboats were little more than armed rowing boats or very small sailing craft, carrying between one and six cannon (normally 6-pounders) on reinforced mountings. Even the smallest navies could afford a few gunboats, and swarms of them guarded all Europe's major seaports, navigable rivers and frontier channels.

Though invaluable as harbour or coastal patrol craft, capable of enforcing their will on unarmed merchant ships or lightly armed privateers, gunboats could seldom be deployed successfully against bigger warships, except in large numbers or against a crippled foe. A single hit from a cannon was usually enough to smash them to pieces, while the inordinate weight of their armament made them difficult to manoeuvre and ensured that they sank almost instantly if holed.

PRIVATEERS

Privateers were essentially licensed pirates. Carrying minimal armament, and with all surplus weight removed, they relied on speed to carry out hit and run raids on helpless merchant ships. If caught, they depended on written government authorizations (known as *lettres de marque*) to protect them from hanging.

Although some armed merchant ships were licensed to take prizes, the British had little need for privateers by the 1790s, and could put crews to better use in regular service, but they were an important means for less potent naval forces to challenge the Royal Navy's control of world trade.

French privateers were particularly numerous and successful. Small enough to operate from harbours inaccessible to warships, and able to maintain their small crews far from major bases, they were a constant menace to British trade wherever it was unprotected by fast sloops or other small warships.

MUSEUM PIECES

The smaller Mediterranean navies still used a variety of old-fashioned ship types as men-of-war, their designs dating back to the Middle Ages. These included single-masted cutters, xebecs and tartans, but the most numerous military throwbacks were galleys.

Single-decked galleys, powered primarily by oars but often equipped with a single sail, offered the advantages of independence from the wind and a very shallow draught, but were slow, fragile and of very limited range. Specialist galleys built by the Swedish and Russian Navies proved useful for inshore operations in the Baltic shallows, but the old oar-drawn vessels of the Turkish, Neapolitan, Venetian and Spanish fleets saw little action and less success.

WEAPONS

Naval weaponry was not particularly specialized, and sailors fought with the same basic tools as ground forces.

Ships, guns were adaptations of standard field and siege designs, with the biggest ships firing long-barrelled 32-pounders, and smaller vessels anything from 2-pounders up. The main difference between land and naval cannon was in the mountings. Shipboard guns were mounted on runners, able to slide back and forth along them, absorbing recoil and allowing the barrels to be 'run' in or out of gunports.

The Royal Navy also made widespread use of light carronades. Short-range cannons with wide, stubby barrels, carronades were hardly used by land forces, but proved highly successful adjuncts to the broadsides of rated warships. Particularly valuable during close range actions, they also functioned as supplementary bow or stern weapons aboard ships-of-the-line. Other navies made limited use of carronades, but none matched the Royal Navy's interest in the weapon, and one British frigate, HMS

This overhead view of ship's cannon shows two guns run out for firing and another inboard for loading, along with the array of ropes and tools needed to secure, clean and load the weapons. Despite their relatively sophisticated mountings, naval guns were far less accurate than their counterparts on land, the pitch and roll of a ship at sea generally rendering careful aim irrelevant. (National Maritime Museum)

Glatton, was equipped only with 56 carronades.

Otherwise the wars were not a time of great technical experimentation, as illustrated by the universal apathy that greeted the American Robert Fulton's 1810 proposals for underwater torpedo craft. Other newfangled devices, like rockets and shrapnel, received only desultory experimental attention, and most of the Navy's wartime efforts to improve its strike power were concerned with gunnery training or safety.

Meanwhile marines carried on fighting with standard muskets, and sailors involved in close combat were issued with a combination of pistols, cutlasses and pikes, although every boarding party contained a few

men armed with muskets and tomahawks, and big ships usually carried a few more sophisticated rifles for sharpshooting from the rigging. Commissioned officers were expected to buy their own blads and pistols, although officers successful in battle often received commemorative swords from patriotic charitable funds.

A carronade. Named after the Carron works in Scotland, where they were developed, carronades were lighter than conventional guns and were deployed on the upper decks of most large British warships. Their rapid fire gave Royal Navy ships a vital advantage during the close-range mélées that ended each of the period's major battles. (National Maritime Museum)

VITAL ELEMENTS

Any armed warship leaving port would be carrying the largest possible quantity of gunpowder (pre-packed into bagged charges) and artillery ammunition.

The vast majority of missiles fired by eighteenth-century warships were simple roundshot. A solid ball of metal, dependent on mass and velocity to cause maximum damage as it smashed into the hull or rigging of its target, roundshot would often pass right through a ship, ripping apart men and spars.

A single ball travelling through the length of a ship could inflict dozens of casualties, but it was extremely difficult to actually sink a large warship with round-shot. If an opponent could not be battered into surrender from a distance, commanders might try grapeshot at close quarters, hoping that the carnage caused by its exploding splinters would end resistance, but incendiary shells represented the best chance of sending an enemy to the bottom.

Commonly called 'carcasses', incendiary shells were packed with flammable material and contained a number of holes for different length fuses, which were lit before firing. Similar shells, fitted with shorter fuses timed to explode in mid-air, were used as flares during night operations.

A warship at sea without enough ammunition might be heading for trouble, but without food or drink it was doomed. Of all the processes that came together to make a fighting navy, the provisioning of ships at sea was the most immediately vital, and the most consistently vexing.

Most Royal Navy provisioning was handled by its Victualling Board, which functioned as a semi-independent bureaucracy, purchasing, testing, packaging and storing goods before selling them on to individual ships' pursers. Ships far from imperial bases would inevitably be forced to replenish supplies from any source available, and pursers (or the captains of small ships with no purser) were entitled to seek full recompense from the Board on their return to a British port. It wasn't always forthcoming, and accounts could take years to settle, but the system worked smoothly enough.

The real problem facing naval provisioners was that, though they recognized the importance of a balanced diet and fresh water in fighting disease, refrigeration and canning remained far in the future. Few foods could be preserved at all, none with absolute certainty that they would remain edible, let alone after weeks at sea. The wartime Navy made strenuous efforts to ensure that it bought healthy food, but could exert only limited control in an unhygienic society, and ships' officers took personal responsibility for accepting or rejecting commodities being loaded aboard.

The diet of a Royal Navy crew at sea could be very interesting after a supply stop in the tropics, but most personnel seem to have preferred the unchanging, and frankly unappetizing, fare provided as rations for ships leaving Britain.

The main staple food was bread, baked into a hard 'biscuit' and inevitably infested with weevils after a short time at sea. Most of the weevils dropped out when the bread was banged against a hard surface, and they were no more than a routine irritant, less threatening than the rats and cockroaches, indefatigable fellow-travellers that took a toll of every ship's supplies.

Other basic ration foods included oatmeal, pease pudding, cheese and butter – or oil for trips to hot regions – along with about six pounds of beef or pork per man per week. The meat could be pickled, in which case it was more likely than not to become contaminated on a long voyage, but it could also be fresh, because every large warship left port with as many cattle, sheep or pigs as could be crammed aboard.

The Victualling Board also supplied quantities of flour, dried fish, raisins, suet and vinegar, along with fresh fruit and vegetables for the early weeks of a voyage whenever possible.

Fresh water was carried, but not as we know it. After a few days at sea, it would be a brackish concoction of pond life, generally green, and sailors did their best to avoid drinking it neat. A gallon of beer a day was provided for men on all but the longest journeys, but they traditionally drank as much as they wanted from the purser's communal beer barrels. If and when the beer ran out, any wine or spirits on board would be added to the water, giving a modicum of protection against its poisons.

Luxury items, or indeed anything not provided for in rations, could only be obtained by private purchase, and although groups of ratings or junior officers might occasionally club together to buy a pig, additional items generally came aboard by one of two routes.

A purser was required to buy clothing, hammocks, candles, cooking fuel (coal or firewood), tobacco and other 'necessaries', and to sell them to the ship's company at a fixed profit. Of course he didn't get the money for months, if it was charged to the pay books of individual seamen, or years if the ship's overall accounts were involved.

The captain of a large man-of-war was by tradition expected to improve the lot of his crew, and his own all-important popularity, by simply buying quantities of luxury items or additional supplies of necessities for distribution at a useful time. For obvious reasons, ordinary men liked serving rich captains.

No vessel in the age of sail dared travel far without a good supply of spare parts, and these were another bulky but crucial element of a warship's baggage. Even without the prospect of combat, the danger of storm damage made it prudent to carry spare sailcloth, ropes and wooden spars.

Some kind of replacement for damaged rigging, masts, decks or hulls could usually be cobbled together once a crippled ship had made land, and the Continental navies were often forced to rely on this, but repair materials could be life-savers for a ship in action. The British could afford to supply this additional insurance, and did so whenever possible.

Big guns, ammunition, provisions, livestock, spare parts ... the bigger the vessel, the more it needed to carry, and the biggest warship in the world wasn't the size of two football pitches. No matter what their class, the Royal Navy's well-stocked fighting ships went to sea quite literally packed to the gunnels, yet somehow they had to find room for the most precious resource of all – people.

A Royal Navy boarding party in action. Forced to skirt anti-boarding nets, the boat crew includes cutlass-wielding sailors and uniformed marines armed with muskets. Led aboard by a lieutenant, they meet a hot reception from defenders using pikes, and the marine falling overboard is probably the victim of a sniper in the rigging. (By John Augustus Atkinson (1775–1833), The Bridgeman Art Library/Stapleton Collection)

CHAPTER THREE

JOLLY TARS
& NAVY BLUES:
MEN OF
HORNBLOWER'S NAVY

I*t took more than just fantastic wealth, centuries of tradition and a unique strategic appreciation of sea power to make an instrument of global Empire. Great fleets of warships were useless without crews, and every large man-of-war needed hundreds of skilled, experienced seamen. Finding them was the wartime Royal Navy's biggest problem.*

Chronic crew shortages crippled many wartime navies, particularly as the size of land armies mushroomed, but their needs were dwarfed by the Royal Navy's. From a peacetime strength of about 15,000 men in 1792, it had expanded eightfold by 1797, and grew more slowly over the next fifteen years to need almost 150,000 sea personnel by 1813.

The tiny elite of part-time politicians that governed Georgian Britain possessed few of the mechanisms for recruiting skilled men on such a scale. Backed by a bureaucracy barely large enough to manage a modern hospital, and drawing on a population only just rising above ten million, it relied on a haphazard combination of coercion, bribery and propaganda.

Mass conscription was politically out of the question in a nation so sure of its theoretical liberties, and anyway produced legions of unskilled cannon-fodder suitable only for the plain carnage of land warfare. Professional seamen could be found among the debtors in prison, or among captured foreign sailors, especially those of nations reluctantly allied to France. Seamen could also be coerced into service by the notorious press gangs, but these much misunderstood

A typical contemporary cartoon portraying the press gang as the enemy of English liberty. Although they provided grist for satirists and often outraged civilian port authorities, press gangs were broadly accepted as the only way to keep the wartime Navy up to strength. Gangs generally adhered to the rule that only professional seamen could to be taken, but regulations exempting those currently employed on another ship were frequently flouted. (By James Gillray, Hulton Getty)

institutions were never able to produce more than a fraction, at most a third, of the Navy's needs at any given time.

Otherwise the government was forced into straight competition for staff with merchant and privateer skippers. The Navy attracted most of its professional recruits by offering a few months' ex gratia pay as a 'bounty' for enlistment, and by tempting them through proclamation or poster with extravagant promises of lavish prize money. The Navy and its captains, who were personally responsible for manning their ships, were at pains to exploit their high reputations, and a famous commander could expect to attract a good many fortune hunters on the strength of his name alone.

Although a few thousand sailors were raised by the Quota Acts of 1795, which required counties and ports to provide a certain number of men for national service, the wartime Navy never found a single solution to its recruitment problems. Its warships invariably went to sea a little short of their full complement, carrying a significant minority of men and boys completely new to life at sea, and it was always more or less desperate for recruits. However, the service muddled through, not only keeping more warships in commission that all its rivals put together, but maintaining levels of crew size, efficiency and fighting capacity that were the envy of Europe.

Volunteer recruitment, supported by bounty payments, actually constituted most of the work done by press gangs ashore, and was the Navy's most reliable source of trained men. This poster enticing men into the Channel Fleet makes no extravagant promises of prize money, but is at pains to name-drop in the hope of attracting recruits back into familiar ships, and includes a threat of compulsion in the small print. (Weidenfeld & Nicolson Archive)

RATINGS

Whether landsman or seaman, volunteer or pressed man, the ordinary sailor did not effectively join the Navy until he was registered on the books of a warship. This occurred after a verbal interview with the ship's first lieutenant, at which point he was either rejected as unfit for service or given a 'rating'.

At the low end of the scale, the under-fifteens could be rated third class boys, and the under-eighteens second class boys, distinct from midshipmen of the first class. Men new to the sea were rated landsmen, and those with enough experience to understand basic duties were rated 'ordinary seaman'. The most prized catch was an 'able seaman', deemed thoroughly familiar with shipboard duties. The best of these might be given petty officer status as soon as he came aboard, especially if a ship was recruiting a hurry.

Ratings were by no means fixed. Any man could work his way up to able seaman in time, a position from which he might well become a petty or warrant officer, and could in theory rise to the very top of the service. Hornblower's era boasted no famous commanders raised from the lower decks, like Captain Cook or Admiral Benbow in earlier decades, but about 120 commissioned officers of the war period were known to have begun their careers as ratings, including a smattering of pressed men.

A rating's career could decline as well as flourish. Petty officers and able seamen could be disrated as a punishment, or because they were no longer fit. They could also lose status simply by being transferred to another ship, something apt to happen at the Admiralty's convenience whether they liked it or not.

Ratings were in theory committed only to their ship, but the practice of arbitrarily 'turning over' men from one ship to another reflected the basic fact that they were chattels of the service for as long as it needed them. Captains were expressly forbidden to discharge men for reasons other than death, illness, permanent incapacity or desertion, all essentially conditions beyond his control.

At the end of his service, any non-commissioned seaman was simply signed off and forgotten, although part of every sailor's pay was deducted to provide for the service hospital at Greenwich.

Ship's boys were allowed on board in regulated numbers, rising to thirteen second class and nineteen third class on the largest warships. They were generally employed as officers' servants before they were fifteen, and

Designed by Wren, the Greenwich maritime hospital supported two or three thousand disabled pensioners, along with a similar number of half-pensioners. They were the only non-commissioned servicemen to receive any kind of formal welfare from the Navy, although senior officers often answered petitions from former shipmates fallen on hard times. (By Samuel Wale (d. 1786), The Bridgeman Art Library, Coram Foundation, London) then given landsmen's duties. Their only real advantage over other landsmen was early experience of conditions at sea, and some remained in that rating for the rest of their careers.

A new landsman might find an immediate niche as an ordinary seaman if his former career had a naval use, but most were not tailors, barbers or experienced personal servants. Others would be given generally unenviable tasks as 'idlers', including a 'captain of the head' to clean the toilets, servants for the gun room and midshipmen's mess, an officers' cook and an unfortunate 'Jack in the Dust' to act as housekeeper to the gun room. Most were destined for dead-end roles as menial deck labour, and unless a wise captain made a point of attaching them to specialist parties for training, they had little chance to learn the many skills needed to make an ordinary seaman.

A competent ordinary seaman was expected to be completely at home with every operational detail of the sails and rigging, as well every conceivable knot, rope trick and aspect of basic ship's maintenance. On or below deck he was capable of performing and understanding all the tasks for routine sailing, storm, calm or combat, and he spoke the arcane language of the sea, for which most contemporaries needed glossaries no less than modern readers. He was inevitably a gymnast, able to dance along a yardarm in a tempest, working at high speed where a landsman could hardly hope to survive.

An able seaman had to do all this and more. Reckoned capable of taking the helm under full sail if necessary, he was expected to understand fully the workings of the main batteries, function as a sailmaker when necessary and perform the vital task of testing the water's depth with the 'lead line'.

A landsman's gross annual pay amounted to a little over £10.60 in 1793, much less after deductions for food, clothing and sundries, while an ordinary seaman was paid £11.30 and an able seaman made about £14. These rates had not changed since Cromwell's day, and were one of the principal grievances behind the great mutinies of 1797, after which pay rises brought an able seaman's wages above £20 per year within a decade.

All ratings messed in the lower decks of a ship, and conditions could be very cramped in a vessel with two or three gun decks. Tables for eating

Big warships operating close to shore were always in danger of running aground, and 'heaving the lead' was the standard means of determining immediate depth. A weighted line was thrown from one or both sides of the bow, and hauled in at regular intervals, when the depth registered was announced in fathoms. Any mistake could be fatal, and the task was only given to trusted able seamen. (By George Cruikshank, Hulton Getty)

This romanticized view of sailors dining aboard ship highlights the gap between popular image and naval reality in Georgian England. Crew meals were indeed taken on the gun decks, but tables were no more than boards slung between cannons, the food was hardly to be lingered over, and a cramped, dingy environment seldom encouraged expansive conviviality. (Hulton Getty)

had to be slung between the guns, and space for hammocks along the sides of decks was at a premium, especially on a ship in port when all the hands slept at the same time.

PETTY OFFICERS

A plethora of intermediate ranks separated the able seaman from commissioned officers. Many were specialist positions calling for proven expertise and filled by the holders of Navy warrants, but most junior NCOs were petty officers, holding their rank solely at the captain's discretion.

Petty officers earned between £20 and £27 pounds a year in 1793, depending on the size of their ship, but the lowest grades received no extra pay before 1806. These included the various 'captains' appointed as foremen for particular parts of the ship. The 'captains of the tops' attended to the foremast and mainmast, and two captains were appointed to the waists, the 'afterguard' and the forecastle.

Rated ships needed between one and four 'yeoman of the sheets', charged with supervising the smooth performance of the fore or aft sails, and three 'yeomen of the stores' guarded stocks belonging to the carpenter, bosun and gunner. A ship's coxswain was the petty officer in charge of steering and maintaining small boats.

The largest group of petty officers were the gunner's mates, who assisted the relatively senior ship's gunner in maintaining the guns, and their direct subordinates the quartergunners, one responsible for every four guns on board. A large ship would carry four gunner's mates and 20–25 quartergunners, and they were often used as a special-purpose platoon when all was quiet with the guns.

Quartermasters were among the more senior petty officers, and were usually very experienced seamen. Their duties included actually taking the wheel, responsibility for the good order of the hold, timekeeping and supervising the flow of provisions from the purser to the crew. Every commissioned ship's crew included at least one quartermaster, and the biggest battleships merited eight. Quartermasters were also given between one and six mates as assistants.

Appointed at the captain's whim, petty officers were generally open to suspicions of acting as spies and informers below decks. The most obvious bearers of the stigma were the feared and often detested bosun's mates, who were important direct instruments of discipline. Bosun's mates administered floggings, and enforced liveliness with their rattan canes or knotted rope-ends, known as 'starters' and only just dropping out of universal use during the wars.

The other principal enforcer of lower deck discipline was the master-at-arms, originally charged with training the company in firearms drill, but functioning as ship's policeman by the late eighteenth century. Every rated warship carried a master-at-arms, with between one and four corporals as assistants, but unrated ships were only given a corporal.

Sometimes a former soldier or marine, the master-at-arms was in fact a warrant officer, his position confirmed by the Navy Board, but was one of several grades that a captain was specifically empowered to disrate on his own authority. This also applied to ship's cooks, who received their warrants in compensation for being disabled in action, and to a number of specialist ranks attached to artisans.

Armed with his 'starter' cane and a suitably dark countenance, the bosun's mate was the captain's enforcer. Though the maximum number of bosun's mates officially permitted was four, and only on first-rate ships, paranoid captains sometimes employed more without attracting criticism from above. (Hulton Getty)

ARTIFICERS

The fragile wooden world of the warship needed constant maintenance and repair, and no ship could sail without its complement of qualified artisans, or 'artificers'. Unfortunately most were not professional seamen and could only be recruited voluntarily, which is why some of the more important craftsmen were granted the status of warrant officers. Like the master-at-arms and the cook, they could be disrated by the captain for serious misconduct, but were generally difficult to replace at short notice.

Carpentry was the artisan skill most often found among seamen, for the obvious reason that it was essential to even the smallest water craft. The ship's carpenter himself was a fairly senior warrant officer, but he was assisted by one or two mates given junior warrants. Because they were responsible for maintaining the structure of the entire ship, they needed a crew of between two and twelve at least semi-skilled workers, rated as petty officers.

The caulker also held a warrant under the carpenter's command. He was responsible for keeping the hull watertight, and replenishing the 'caulking' tar that filled the gaps between planks.

The British public's somewhat misplaced belief in a sense of order in naval affairs is again reflected in this patriotic tribute to the Navy's artisans. Though craftsmen were absolutely vital to the maintenance of wooden warships, neither Britannia nor the Navy provided any formal mechanism for their training or recruitment, relying instead on the incentive of the warrant officer rank to entice skilled men from a volatile job market ashore. (Hulton Getty)

Both the sailmaker and the ropemaker were warrant officers subordinate to the bosun. Sailmakers supervised delivery, inspection, maintenance and repair of all their materials with the help of a mate and one or two crew, but manufacture of ropes was a one-man job, though both departments could call on parties of able seamen when the need arose.

Frigates and ships-of-the-line carried a warranted armourer, and one or two armourer's mates, while smaller vessels relied on a mate alone. They were generally responsible for upkeep of all the ship's metalwork, working from a portable forge, but crew small arms were their prime concern.

Coopers were needed for barrels, but not very often. Though petty officers, they and their mates were paid as able seamen, spending much of their time filling in on other duties. They frequently helped the steward, another relatively lowly non-seaman who distributed provisions on the purser's behalf.

A steward was less likely to rise to the precarious heights of purser than the captain's clerk, the one person on board ship whose duties were purely secretarial, although literate landsmen might be employed informally as writers for the officers. Often fairly young and liable to gentlemanly pretensions, the clerk was frequently lodged in the midshipmen's berth.

Four 'captain's servants' were officially allowed for every hundred men on a ship's books, but many captains carried fewer. A euphemism for well-bred boys too young to be midshipmen, they became genuine personal staff after regulations were changed in 1794.

The wardroom or gun-room staff included one or two cooks, and up to three wardroom servants, while commissioned officers and the three 'standing' warrant officers were each allowed one personal attendant.

Women also travelled aboard warships, and were present in numbers at all the major battles of the era, when they were usually drafted as assistants to the surgeon. Most were the wives of officers and NCOs, but the rules governing soldiers also allowed each company of marines to travel with five women.

WARRANT OFFICERS

Lieutenants and above received their commissions from the Admiralty, while midshipmen and petty officers earned their rank at the captain's pleasure, but warrant officers were appointed by the Navy Board, the all-embracing administrative branch of the service that governed its supply and logistic requirements. Apart from the relatively lowly status granted to artisans, masters-at-arms and cooks, there were three broad grades of warrant officer in the wartime Royal Navy.

The senior group were essentially men from the officer class. Entitled to walk the quarterdeck, their status was almost that of commissioned officers, and their most senior figure was the ship's master.

A naval technician at the top of his profession, the master earned slightly more than a lieutenant, but provided his own charts and navigation instruments. Though he enjoyed accommodation privileges equivalent to the first lieutenant, and was perhaps the most practically important man aboard, he was not treated like a commissioned officer in terms of half-pay or prisoner rights.

The master was responsible for piloting and navigation, and worked in close personal liaison with the captain, keeping him precisely informed of position and conditions. His other duties included responsibility for liquor, ballast, general weight distribution and the ship's practical fitness above decks.

Literacy was a basic requirement for any warrant officer, and the master wrote the ship's operational log book, which was often the sole source for the captain's own log. As well as details of the voyage and the ship's condition, the master's log was expected to record depths and currents, as well as interesting coastlines. Along with theft from foreign ships, it remained the Navy's principal source of new information for maps and charts.

Chaplains and surgeons, professional men in civilian life, enjoyed recognition as gentlemen, and usually messed with the commissioned officers. Chaplains had been regarded as almost entirely superfluous in the earlier eighteenth century, but enjoyed something of a wartime revival, and from 1812 could expect half pay after eight years' service. It was still difficult to recruit chaplains, and only 79 were serving with the Navy in 1814, most of them with the more prestigious vessels.

The Navy employed about 550 surgeons in 1793, and most were by reputation drunken incompetents. By 1815 their numbers had risen to 850, and an improvement in general standards was linked to pay rises (eventually giving a surgeon almost £200 per year), the establishment of half-pay and the Navy's decision to fund at least some shipboard medical supplies. Their mates, renamed 'surgeon's assistants' after 1805, were rated as petty officers, and might be completing naval training to become surgeons. They were

As this caricature suggests, ships' pursers epitomised the common man's mistrust of the entrepreneur. They were almost universally suspected of giving short measures and otherwise making an illegal profit out of sailors' basic necessities, but the Navy's provisioning regulations were sufficiently labyrinthine to make detection difficult. (By Thomas Rowlandson, Hulton Getty)

more often simple orderlies, and most surgeons reached the Navy fully trained.

The other warrant officer treated like a gentleman was the purser. Recruited from captain's clerks or the secretaries of admirals at sea, pursers were entirely responsible for purchase, maintenance, resale and distribution of all the goods aboard a ship. Most but not all were purchased from the Navy, and the purser depended on good credit, leaving a bond as security for goods worth as much as £1,200 for a large battleship.

Pursers were ill-paid, earning no more than a bosun or gunner, but were given a bonus of £25 at the end of each year in service and expected to make a profit on transactions with the crew. Though it was never stated in regulations, they were entitled to keep an eighth of most basic goods sold to their shipmates – and between five and ten per cent of clothing, tobacco and other listed commodities.

The detested 'fourteen ounce pound' provided profit and a measure of security against wastage, but the purser needed to stay right on top of his accounts to keep bankruptcy at bay. He also had good reason to keep a vigilant eye on the way goods were stored, and to be constantly on his guard against wastage through casual over-use or predators, both animal and human.

Even after their eighth was taken away in the wake of the 1797 mutinies, most pursers seem to have achieved modest prosperity and made themselves deeply unpopular in the process. Almost universal suspicion of fraud was often intensified by the close relationship between captain and purser, who would sometimes share the risk and profit of purchasing supplies from foreign ports on long voyages.

The second rank on the social scale of warrant holders was occupied by master's and surgeon's mates, who messed in the gun room (or the midshipmen's berths) and might one day hope to emulate their wardroom superiors. This group could also include the shadowy figure of the schoolmaster, employed by some ships to teach prospective officers mathematics, navigation and the basics of literacy. Paid at midshipman rates, they seem to have been a sorry collection of last-chancers, even more prone to drunkenness than cooks or surgeons.

The last group of warrant officers comprised a warship's three 'standing officers', so called because they stayed with a ship even after it was decommissioned, often moving in with their families once it was laid up in dock.

The ship's carpenter was the only standing officer who was generally trained on land, usually learning histrade as a shipwright before serving the mandatory six months at sea as a mate. By 1808 he had become the highest paid of them, earning about £70 per year aboard a three-decker. The carpenter's busiest times came at the beginning of a ship's commission, when his crew had to build all the on-board fittings, and in the aftermath of combat, when he worked flat out to make emergency repairs and remake the bulwarks broken down to clear the gun decks.

The ship's gunner was primarily a maintenance official, since artillery in action was controlled by lieutenants. Expected to have served four years at sea, and at least one as a petty officer, a gunner had to pass a rudimentary mathematical examination, putting him on a pay scale rising to about £58 per year after 1808. Gunners and their crews of petty officers manufactured the breeches, tackles and other artillery accessories, packed cartridges and looked after the ship's supply of gunpowder. Their overriding concern was to ensure that a ship's guns were ready for action at any moment, and much of the routine work involved running regular checks on their condition.

Most bosuns (or boatswains) had had once been able seamen, and all had spent at least a year as a petty officer. The bosun was hardly a specialist, but was a figure of genuine authority and paid at the same rate as a gunner. Backed by his posse of mates, he took direct care of all the aspects of ship's wellbeing that were the master's responsibility, and was the ship's disciplinary supremo. Bosuns were inevitably high-profile characters, usually distinguished by volcanic vocal chords, and many earned reputations for brutality or drunkenness.

Bosuns and their mates were also responsible for issuing the 'calls' that echoed around a ship. Using a small horn and a cupped hand to produce a scale of high-pitched piping sounds, they announced a sum-mons to action, the start of the day or a number of other standard procedures.

OFFICERS – A VERY BRITISH CLASS

Hornblower's Navy was never short of officers, and maintained hundreds on half pay at any given time, partly because it didn't need that many. The full crew of a standard British ship-of-the-line, as many as eight hundred men, was run by a captain and five lieutenants. They could not hope to maintain efficient control against such odds without an element of crew consent, and unless they were essentially good at their jobs.

Most navies by 1790 were desperately short of men able to run a ship or exercise effective authority, but British society was unique in producing a corps of professional naval officers coherent and efficient enough to wield global power. In Spain or pre-Revolutionary France command belonged exclusively to a narrow caste of hereditary nobles, but Royal Navy officers were drawn from a much more usefully vague class of 'gentlemen'. High rank was open to the titled, the wealthy and even, given sufficient luck and patronage, to talented members of an expanding middle class.

This helped make the Navy a career of choice for the aristocracy's younger brothers and the respectable children of humbler families, as did a shortage of other options. The social status of the Church and the Army had been falling for decades, academics were still glorified servants, and powerful men became lawyers rather than the other way round. For an aspiring young man without investment capital, the Navy offered about the best chance of fame or fortune.

And then there was the romance. Many young boys from well-heeled families evidently longed for a roving, precarious existence aboard an overcrowded, rat-infested death-trap. Aside from the naïve militarism to which young boys incline, this reflected the glamour attached to a successful service. Regardless of personal status or achievement, a commissioned officer in the King's Navy shared the aura of its prestige and reputation for invincibility.

So a bustling, competitive sample of Britain's élite and would-be élite classes went to sea as boys, and many became lifelong sailors. Those from relatively undistinguished backgrounds, and without 'interest' in high places, could hardly expect the same fast-track treatment as the sons of admirals and peers, but might just win it by a combination of skill, luck and judicious diplomacy. Nelson's father was after all a Norfolk country parson, and Horatio Hornblower was the orphaned son of a village apothecary.

MIDSHIPMAN – SPRINGBOARD TO GLORY?

Young gentlemen entering the Navy in wartime, when career prospects were at their brightest, might go to sea as eight- or nine-year-olds, gaining early experience as 'captain's servants', but were not generally rated midshipman before the age of fifteen.

A midshipman's precise rank, like so much Navy administration, was only vaguely defined. Though technically no better than a warrant officer and paid less than most (£22.50 per year), status among the officer class was implicitly recognized in his operational duties, and made explicit when warrant officers were occasionally punished for offences against midshipmen as 'superior officers'.

A ship-of-the-line might employ as many as sixteen 'middies', the importance of seniority sharply defined in the crowded confines of their mess, but small sloops or other light craft often sailed with only one. New midshipmen were supposed to undergo training by experienced personnel, but though a good learner could achieve basic all-round competence in a few months on a well-run ship, the best-intentioned youngster might never rise above the rudiments of bullying and drunkenness in an unhappy crew.

A midshipman's duty was primarily to assist lieutenants in executive control of the crew, and sometimes to take their place when insufficient commissioned officers were available. During any kind of action, midshipmen were responsible for subdivisions of guns or other small fighting units, but also served on the quarterdeck as aides to the senior officers. A trusted or promising midshipman might take command of small boat parties, and even a prize crew if no lieutenant could be spared.

Senior midshipmen were often given extra responsibility as master's mates. Sometimes allowed to mess with the warrant officers in the gun room, they acted as sub-lieutenants, and might become acting

This is the way a midshipman was supposed to look – a well-heeled young man, fully equipped with the tools of his trade, and on the threshold of a long career as a commissioned officer. His type certainly existed, and many rich or well-connected young 'middies' soon made the leap to lieutenant, but hard-up has-beens in their thirties were at least equally common. (By Thomas Rowlandson, Hulton Getty) lieutenants if a position fell vacant while they were still awaiting a commission.

Regulations required candidates for promotion to be at least twenty years old, with six years at sea, not necessarily in the Navy, and at least two years as a midshipman or master's mate. A royal dispensation could promote a midshipman who had not done his time, and a great deal of cheating also took place on behalf of the well-connected, most frequently by captains entering boys on the lists for several years before they actually went to sea.

Applicants for a commission were required to pass a fairly rigorous oral test in seamanship before an examining board of five senior officers (or three on foreign stations). Success might take several attempts, and hardly meant automatic promotion unless a midshipman had good connections. Someone like Hornblower, entirely without social or professional patrons, might wait for years unless an opportunity to excel arose, and most midshipmen's messes were dominated by men in their twenties and thirties, some even in their fifties.

LIEUTENANT – A CAREER FOR LIFE

Lieutenants were the most junior commissioned officers in the Navy, and all earned about £100 per year by the early nineteenth century, regardless of seniority or ship size. The crew of every commissioned warship contained at least one lieutenant, and they commanded the Navy's unrated craft. Most sloops carried a single lieutenant as executive to the commander, but a first-rate ship-of-the-line could accommodate six.

A commission brought the basic security of half pay for life, although it only approached the full fifty per cent for those with the longest service, and the right to inhabit a ship-of-the-line's wardroom (or the gun room in a smaller ship). Their elevated social status was recognized even in captivity, when a lieutenant could expect courteous treatment and acceptance of his word as parole.

In the normal course of operational routine, lieutenants stood watch duties, taking responsibility for all or part of the crew on a shift basis. This all-important vigil was a relatively comfortable responsibility on a large warship, but officers on small sloops could only delegate the duty to ship's masters and more junior officers.

Most lieutenants were stationed on the gun decks when in action, commanding a 'division' of all or some of the guns along one side of a warship. They could also expect to command boarding parties, shore raids, recruitment details, cutting-out operations and prize crews.

Although date of commission decided the ranking order of lieutenants on a particular ship, seniority had little bearing on further promotion, except that first lieutenants enjoyed the best opportunities for success in the field, and so on down the list.

The first lieutenant of any ship, but particularly a large man-of-war, occupied a unique and in many ways hazardous position. The captain's executive on the quarterdeck, and primarily responsible for the crew's overall efficiency, he could expect to be the focus of any disciplinary problems, whether as the mainspring of tyranny or as the only man who was legitimately empowered to replace the captain.

In the event of a captain's death or manifest incapacity, a first lieutenant usually took charge with a heavy heart. His position implied no permanent elevation, and his actions were likely to be scrutinized in minute detail once he reached a home port. If the captain was dead, he knew a single blameworthy error could end all hope of promotion, and if the captain was still alive he stood a good chance of being ruined at the inevitable court-martial.

COMMANDER – FIRST TASTE OF POWER

The intermediate rank between lieutenant and captain, now generally called a lieutenant commander, was known as a 'master and commander' until the early nineteenth century, and then simply as a commander. In practice commanders were usually addressed as 'captain', and they were captains in terms of responsibilities and work load.

The commander at sea was likely to be on detached duty, and shared the loneliness common to full captains with few of the compensatory luxuries. In particular, his privacy was restricted to a tiny cabin in the appallingly cramped conditions of the Navy's little warships. On the other hand fast sloops were ideally equipped to take prizes along the trade routes that were their hunting grounds, so that bold commanders were often able to augment their £200 per year salaries and secure the relative wealth they would need as post captains.

Promotion between lieutenant and admiral was largely a matter of ship size, and a commander became a post captain automatically on receiving appointment to fifth-rater or higher. Some lieutenants moved straight to post rank, but it was rare to be promoted over the head of an available commander.

POST CAPTAIN –
TOUGH AT THE TOP

Some things about captaincy never change. Especially in wartime, it is and always will be a position of loneliness and potentially crushing responsibility. During Hornblower's wars, when Royal Navy captains fought the elements, disease and half Europe in great, cumbersome sailing ships, it was also a position of considerable social prestige.

As a post captain, a man could hope for prize money and a good marriage ashore. He might also expect to end his days as a justice of the peace or, if he won public renown, a member of parliament. But honour in Georgian society came encumbered by a welter of economic responsibilities, and they began to bite as soon as a captain took control over his wooden world.

A good captain needed seamanship, initiative, courage, luck, a gift for authority and a balanced mind. These and good social contacts would help him attract a 'following' of officers and seamen, without which finding a competent crew might prove impossible in wartime.

His next problem, presenting

The port admiral entertaining officers aboard ship at Portsmouth. Life on his ship could be extremely comfortable for a wealthy captain or admiral. Little wonder that some officers were reluctant to risk their floating hotels in action, or that poor captains would sometimes do almost anything to secure a prize. (By Thomas Rowlandson, The Bridgeman Art Library/British Library, London)

enormous difficulties for a poor man like Hornblower, was financing his promotion. A captain needed money and credit to provide the tools of his trade, expensive braided uniforms, weapons and furniture for his cabin. He was also expected to buy at least a few small luxuries for the crew as a whole, and needed ready funds to pay enlistment bounties or buy supplies from foreign ports.

These expenses were reclaimed from the Navy at the end of each voyage, but settlement could take years and not all claims were accepted, so that many captains found themselves promoted into debt. On the other hand many captains were born rich, rising effortlessly above such petty expenses, and a single valuable prize might keep any officer comfortable for life.

Once at sea, a captain's lifestyle reflected his financial status. The captain could bring whatever he liked on board, and space could be found for almost anything at his behest, so that some cabins were veritable palaces, laden with silver, silks and art works, their tables groaning with the captain's delicacies.

The captain's rule over his ship at sea was a personal affair that defied generalization, but it in many ways resembled a medieval monarch's shaky absolutism – omnipotent and aloof, but depending on the tacit consent of most subjects. The best captains, like Pellew or Nelson, were inspiring leaders, and the wartime Navy employed fewer incompetents or sadistic tyrants than is sometimes imagined.

With exceptions, such as the junior flag captains selected by admirals, promotion within the rank was determined by size of ship, as was a pay scale rising to almost £400 a year (from 1808) for the captain of a first-rate. A captain's ultimate promotion to admiral was determined solely by his date of commission to post rank. Unless he managed to achieve dismissal from the Navy altogether, usually either for fiddling the accounts or blatant dereliction of duty, only death could prevent his eventual elevation to rear-admiral.

COMMODORE – MAN OF THE HOUR

The title of commodore was the Navy's way of ensuring that incompetent admirals were never given active employment, and that the best captains were given the most important work in the field. Commodores were given temporary command of squadrons or other operational units, hoisting a broad pennant aboard their ships to distinguish them as local commanders-in-chief, and became captains again when their mission was complete. Those chosen for fron-line work were usually regarded as the best and brightest, and could expect to hoist their pennant regularly until promotion to admiral became feasible.

OPPOSITE

An old commodore relives past glories. The temporary distinction of a commodore's pennant could not hasten a captain's promotion to admiral. Nelson had been a captain for eighteen years when he became a rear-admiral in 1797, and Hornblower eventually became a rear-admiral in 1821, when all those above him on the captain's list had either died or retired. (Hulton Getty)

ADMIRAL –
SURVIVAL OF THE FITTEST

The wartime Royal Navy was never short of admirals, and the service was always hopelessly overloaded with them in peacetime, but few ever hoisted their flags on active service. The Admiralty's main method of keeping surfeit and seniority under control was to turn promotion into a form of retirement, and many senior captains happily became rear-admirals 'of the yellow' on the understanding that they were permanently restricted to half pay.

An admiral at sea was something of an event, generally travelling with a considerable entourage, including servants, secretaries, a selection of naval protégés and sometimes a personal signals officer. Concerned with larger issues, he usually left control over the flagship to its captain, traditionally the most junior in any fleet, promoted to ship-of-the-line status as the admiral's choice. All the same, his presence inevitably dominated proceedings, bringing a stream of visiting officers and dignitaries on board, and turning the ship into something of a social centre.

The prize system gave a commander-in-chief a generous portion of every treasure captured by his forces, and admirals on foreign stations could afford a highly extravagant lifestyle yet still come home greatly enriched. The same did not apply to the more humble commanders of obscure shore stations, but all admirals were well paid by the standards of the day.

The arcane ranking system among admirals dated from the Commonwealth Navy of the 1650s, when the service operated as a single fleet, divided into three divisions of three squadrons. Active rear-admirals were still designated of the Blue, White or Red divisions, in ascending order of seniority, as were the vice-admi-

rals who functioned as theatre commanders for the Georgian Navy. Full admirals, usually too old for sea commands, were either of the Blue or White until 1805, when the title Admiral of the Fleet was adopted to distinguish the Navy's most senior officer.

Peace tended to keep established field commanders in the most important posts well into old age, so that men like Howe, the Hood brothers and Hotham were well past their prime when they took command of British fleets during the early 1790s. It took several years of war to bring a younger generation of more aggressive leaders to the fore, but even in 1814 there were sea commands for less than a quarter of the active admirals available. Stagnation returned once the wars ended, and only those with serious political clout could hope for employment in a dramatically shrunken service that boasted 75 rear-admirals in 1816.

Admiral Howe, the victor of the First of June battle in 1794, shows his age as he is rewarded by George III. Strict seniority regulations and prolonged peace had left the Navy's highest commands in the hands of old, tired men by the early 1790s. The most vigorous of them, Howe was in his late sixties when the wars broke out, and had collapsed from exhaustion before the end of the battle. (By Isaac Cruikshank, The Bridgeman Art Library/Guildhall Art Gallery, Corporation of London)

MARINES

Junior marine officers outside their divisional barracks. Marines ashore were organized like a conventional land division, but were regarded as second-class soldiers by the Army. Once at sea they faced all the dangers of life aboard a warship, and bore the brunt of close-quarters fighting wherever it took place, but were again accorded very low social status. (Circa 1830–37, by L. Mansion and St. Eschauzier, The Bridgeman Art Library/The Stapleton Collection)

Companies of British Army troops sailed aboard all warships, usually commanded by a captain of marines, who was the ranking and prize share equivalent of a naval lieutenant. Marine captains were sometimes assisted by an army lieutenant, but sergeants were much more common seconds-in-command, and led the marines aboard small warships.

The proportion of marines aboard a serving warship edged up during the war years, so that by 1815 about twenty per cent of a large ship's crew were soldiers. They joined a ship as it was fitting out from the nearest marine barracks, where they were organized into divisions and companies along land army lines.

Marines were intended to act as infantry during shore operations, but also functioned as the officers' main defence against mutiny. During sea combats they joined boarding parties, were stationed around the upper decks as snipers or guards for the captain, and fought the guns alongside regular seamen.

Drilled and disciplined as troops, and dressed in full uniform where contemporary seamen had none, marines formed a largely separate shipboard community, and were generally treated by qualified seamen with a scorn otherwise reserved for idlers.

TEAM SPIRIT

The diverse social and professional population of a British warship had little in common, but many of the crews manning Hornblower's Navy developed a cohesion and *esprit de corps* that made them difficult to break up and fearsome enemies in a sea fight. That bonding was born of the shared endeavour, hardship and danger that distinguished their day-to-day life in the 'steep tub' they called home.

CHAPTER FOUR

LIFE AND DEATH ON THE OCEAN WAVES

A man-of-war at anchor in port was hardly at rest. Sailors were kept busy with repairs, drilling, shore patrols and constant attention to the ship's appearance. Upper decks were scrubbed every day and lower decks once a week, though only if the weather were dry enough to prevent the spread of damp. The ship's paintwork, metalwork and rigging were kept in exhibition trim, and a captain whose vessel was part of an anchored fleet could expect any failure of outward presentation to bring down the admiral's wrath or scorn.

Not all this activity was strictly necessary, but it kept crews occupied. The regular rigging and gunnery contests held within fleets or particular ships were useful training exercises, but were also recognized as a means to keep seamen happy without resort to the demons of strong liquor or shore leave.

Any commander sending large numbers of men off on leave could expect trouble, either from their carousing activities or large-scale desertion, while keeping all the men on board was asking for frustrations to boil over into disobedience. Generally speaking, captains, who were required to live on board themselves for as long as a ship was in commission, tended to dangle shore leave as a prize for a well-behaved few.

Visiting other ships was less difficult all round. Ratings would occasionally be sent round the fleet to perform executions or other ceremonials, and social visits were not uncommon during free time for officers and men. Captains were also in demand for attendance at the admiral's table, examination boards and courts-martial.

For the majority of ratings stuck on board ship, with a little time and at least part of their wages on their hands, the boatloads of prostitutes and peddlers that pulled alongside each day and night provided vital leisure

A first-rate taking in stores. Few of the crew were allowed ashore when a large man-of-war was in port, but the port could come to the ship. These boats are engaged in private trade, either as 'market boats' selling legitimate provisions, or as less scrupulous traders in pressed recruits, loose women or alcohol. (By Joseph Mallord William Turner (1775–1851), The Bridgeman Art Library/Cecil Higgins Art Gallery, Bedford)

outlets. Civilian visitors to the lower decks could come on board if passed by the bosun, who acted as the ship's unofficial customs official. Most captains turned a blind eye to the mass adoption of temporary 'wives', and the most strenuous efforts to prevent strong spirits from reaching the men were usually in vain.

The relative ease of life in port was shattered the moment orders to sail arrived. The business of rounding up or replacing crewmen, of completing repairs, fixtures and fittings, and of loading aboard provisions or equipment kept everybody at full stretch until it was done. Recruitment was rarely complete before a ship was otherwise ready for sea, and the rush of activity would sometimes be followed by a prolonged lull, but fitting out was generally the immediate prelude to a radical change of lifestyle for everyone on the ship's list.

ON WATCH – AT SEA

The vast majority of the time a ship was at sea it was simply battling the elements, sailing along on patrol, blockade, convoy or other duties. The sight of a strange sail was rare enough, and months could pass without the sudden surge of combat, so that a sailor's life at sea was usually run

A crew and its women at leisure on the main deck of a warship in port. Most captains allowed their ships to resemble floating taverns when in harbour – because the alternatives were either discontent aboard or mass desertion from shore leave – but officers and marines were on hand to prohibit violence and detect illicit strong liquor. (By Thomas Sutherland, National Maritime Museum) according to an exhausting and repetitive routine.

Any ship that was seriously under-manned or short of skilled crew was in peril from the moment it left harbour, and the captain's first job was efficient distribution of the labour he had. As soon as everyone was aboard, the senior officers would begin work on lists marking down the precise duties of every man.

The process would begin by dividing all the crew except for idlers, who worked land hours, into 'watches'. Though a few captains experimented with three watches, most felt the need to keep half the crew on duty at all times, dividing it into starboard and larboard groups (port was not officially adopted for 'left' until 1844). The night was divided into four watch periods. The first 'dog-watch' of two hours ran from six until eight, followed by full four-hour watches and a second dog-watch, ending at six in the morning, a system that kept everybody's sleeping hours in rotation.

Once split into watches, crewmen were allocated particular tasks during normal operations, along with positions when the ship was at 'general quarters' (action stations) or performing one of a number of set manoeuvres. The stations of officers, petty officers and idlers were predetermined, but there was a pecking order for the positions allotted to ratings.

The best mature seamen would usually be stationed on deck at the forecastle, where they would work the anchors, foresail, jib and bowsprit. Next in precedence were the agile young 'topmen' assigned to the rigging, who worked the heavy cables and the capstan when on deck. The 'after-guard', generally populated by ordinary seamen, handled the braces from behind the mainmast, and the lowly 'waisters' in the centre of the deck were often landsmen, primarily occupied in hauling ropes to control the mainsails, pumping out the bilges, handling livestock and other menial work.

MANPOWER!

Crew deployment aboard a 42-gun frigate during routine day-time sailing. This example shows a vessel with its full compliment of officers and men, but wartime post captains expected to sail at least a little understrength, and recruitment problems forced some to leave port with little more than skeleton crews. The exact proportion of landsmen and boys to able and ordinary seamen varied considerably from ship to ship, and according to circumstances aboard individual vessels. Most captains were obliged to place some inexperienced men among the specialist crews in the tops, and wise commanders did so as a means of training new specialists.
(By W. F. Mitchell, Hulton Getty)

CREWING OF
THE 42 GUN FRIGATE

FORE TOPMEN
Starboard watch	1 Petty Officer
	10 Ordinary and able seamen
	1 Landsman
Larboard watch	1 Petty Officer
	10 Ordinary and able seamen
	1 Landsman

MAIN TOPMEN
Starboard watch	1 Petty Officer
	11 Ordinary and able seamen
	1 Landsmen
Larboard watch	1 Petty Officer
	11 Ordinary and able seamen
	1 Landsman

MIZZEN TOPMEN
Starboard watch	1 Petty Officer
	6 Ordinary and able seamen
	1 Landsman
	1 Boy
Larboard watch	1 Petty Officer
	6 Ordinary and able seamen
	1 Landsman
	1 Boy

FORECASTLE MEN
Starboard watch	1 Petty Officer
	10 ordinary and able seamen
	3 Landsman
Larboard watch	1 Petty Officer
	10 Ordinary and able seamen
	3 Landsman

WAISTERS
Starboard watch	1 Petty Officer
	3 Ordinary and able seaman
	12 Landsmen
Larboard watch	1 Petty Officer
	2 Ordinary and able seamen
	5 Landsmen

AFTERGUARD
Starboard watch	1 Petty Officer
	4 Ordinary and able seamen
	13 Landsmen
Larboard watch	1 Petty Officer
	2 Ordinary and able seamen
	11 Landsmen

IDLERS	4 Petty officers
	7 Ordinary and able seamen
	7 Landsmen
	8 Artisans
SERVANTS	12
MARINES	4 Marine Officers
	21 Marine Privates
	27 Marine NCOs
BOATSWAIN'S MATES	4 Petty Officers
QUARTERMASTERS	6 Petty Officers
GUNNER'S CREW	12 Petty Officers
CARPENTER'S CREW	10 Artisans
OFFICERS	5 Commissioned Officers
	5 Seamen warrant officers
	10 Civilian warrant officers
	12 Mates and midshipmen

TOTAL	306 CREW

SEA DAYS

Until the rules were changed in 1805, the day of a ship at sea began officially at noon, so that the logs would register morning battles as taking place on the previous day. In practical terms, the day began whenever the captain said it did, but that was usually at four in the morning, when the last dog-watch began.

As the new watch was roused, followed by the idlers, the quartermasters at the wheel would change over, as would the lookouts covering every horizon (often midshipmen or boys with sharp young eyes). The ship's course was checked, and the log was trailed in the water to gauge its

Whenever danger threatened, the vital task of lookout duty was entrusted to those young men with the sharpest eyes. In quiet or friendly waters, the duty was often meted out as punishment, and unfortunate midshipmen like this sorry specimen could expect to endure many a hangover on a forlorn vigil among the winds and ropes. (by George Cruikshank, Hulton Getty)

speed, while the carpenter's and bosun's crews examined the ship for holes and leaks.

Regardless of the time it occurred, every British warship met the dawn at action stations. General quarters was called at least fifteen minutes before first light, bringing every member of the crew on deck and into his assigned combat position. Once full daylight had revealed, as it usually did, that all was quiet to the horizons, the crew could go back to working or sleeping. Only then were the cooks allowed to light the galley fire, which had to be put out whenever the guns were readied for action.

Regardless of sailing requirements, dawn began the day-long process of adjusting sheets and rigging by small amounts as a means of reducing wear and tear. Otherwise the first jobs for the new watch were cleaning the decks, sails, metalwork and any furniture or personal effects marked for scrubbing that day. Getting clothing clean wasn't easy without fresh water, and crews made use of the only ammoniac substance readily available – urine stored in a tub – before rinsing their garments in sea water. Bathing was generally regarded as a dangerous activity risked only by eccentrics.

Sometime after six the sleeping watch would be recalled, so that the entire crew was now on duty for the day. In warm climates, an awning would be stretched across the quarterdeck at about this time, screening officers, wheel operatives and signallers from the heat.

The ship's company would be called to breakfast for half an hour from around eight. This might include oat gruel or a little butter and cheese (usually rancid), but primarily consisted of hard biscuit, washed down with 'coffee' made from burnt biscuit crumbs. Either before or after breakfast, the whole crew attended to personal cleaning, stowing hammocks and clearing the lower decks – a process than could be drilled down below ten minutes on a competitively run ship.

Maintenance and drill then filled most of the daylight hours, with sails and guns being exercised and the marines paraded. The work was punctuated by 'divisions' some time after nine-thirty, when the crew would parade for inspection, and by the day's first tot of grog shortly before lunch. Most of the midshipmen would be expected to join the captain in using a sextant to estimate the ship's latitude by 'taking the noon sight', and lunch followed almost immediately, lasting as long as 90 minutes on some ships.

The afternoon's work would climax with a second grog ration at four, after which supper would last for 45 minutes. From that point the evening routine began to mirror the morning, with another call to action stations as darkness fell, and by six the first watch would be back in its hammocks. Emergencies and 'dawn quarters' apart, the crew could expect to rest undisturbed when off watch, though the captain himself might choose to be woken and informed of any significant change in the ship's circumstances.

In detail, these routines were a matter for individual captains, and they were anyway mutable depending on circumstances. A ship with a fleet might spend time on manoeuvres, and a convoy escort was often forced to observe the routines of its merchant charges as a matter of convenience. A ship on patrol might be called upon to inspect neutral merchantmen for contraband, and any kind of storm dispensed with any need for training work. Even extreme calm could disrupt routines, sometimes forcing crews to man the rowboats and tow a warship for hours on end.

SIGNALLING

Sending messages by hoisting flags was a vital aspect of operations whenever a warship was in company with other vessels. Until the 1790s, when Captain Home Popham came up with the vastly improved system of listing full words and individual letters as flag combinations, codes had consisted of a number of set phrases, leaving acres of room for misinterpretation and ruining many a fleet action.

Complete with scrambling flags to confuse enemies, Popham's system allowed captains and admirals to say anything they liked to each other provided they were in eyeshot, and made an enormous difference to operational efficiency.

THE PERMANENT BATTLE

Even on the luckiest and most sanitary warship, at least five per cent of crew was likely to die during a long commission in foreign waters, and Navy slang employed a bewildering variety of euphemisms for death. Battle was too rare to account for more than about three per cent of wartime fatalities. The real killers at sea were disease and accident, with the former winning hands down.

The British paid a lot more attention to sanitation than most of their rivals. By the 1790s they had learned to fight scurvy with fresh food, and to take quarantine very seriously, but their crews still faced innumerable exotic contagions in the sure knowledge that contemporary medicine provided no effective protection against any of them.

Though crowded ships were excellent breeding grounds for disease, going ashore was even more dangerous on overseas service. Malaria was inevitable in the tropics, and yellow fever could decimate a ship in days, but crews were struck down with almost equal regularity in northern Europe and the Mediterranean. Though some killers were identified as typhus or bubonic plague, most were simply labelled as 'fever'.

An anniversary celebration of Nelson's victory at Trafalgar, produced by the Boy's Own Paper *in 1885. Nelson's famous eloquence before Trafalgar would have been impossible without the new Popham flag codes, even if the need for speed did force him to substitute 'expects' for 'confides', a word without a single numerical equivalent. (By Walter William May (1831–96), The Bridgeman Art Library/Private Collection)*

The most frequent cause of accidental death was a fall from the rigging, either through storm, haste or carelessness, but foul weather could pitch men overboard or crush them under ill-secured guns, and almost any minor accident could result in death from blood poisoning.

Shipboard funerals were almost a matter of routine, treated with understandable solemnity by the living of all ranks, and crews resented any failure to observe ceremonial. The most infamous single-ship mutiny of the war years, aboard the frigate *Hermione* in September 1797, took place after the brutal Captain Pigot tossed the bodies of two men killed in rigging accidents over the side. He and the officers were killed before the crew turned themselves over to Spanish authorities in what is now Venezuela, but the ship was later recaptured by a cutting-out operation, and most of the mutineers were hanged.

STRONG MEDICINE – MUTINY

A deathly hush surrounds the modern idea of mutiny, so heinous and exceptional seems the crime, but it was regarded as commonplace in Hornblower's Navy, and around a thousand mutinies took place during the wars, many of them resolved without recourse to legal action.

The numbers reflect a Georgian concept of mutiny covering offences that fell well short of actually seizing a ship. Most of the cases tried by the Navy were for individual misconduct, which could include mutinous language, holding mutinous gatherings and concealing other people's offences. The Navy also treated striking a senior officer or the remotest sympathy with republicanism as tantamount to mutiny.

Any kind of mutiny was punishable by death, but the Navy allowed itself the discretion to imprison, flog or pardon instead. This reflected an understanding that mutiny was sometimes justified by officer cruelty, and that seamen were easily led. Ringleaders with radical pretensions could expect execution, but occasionally an entire crew would have its demands met and no official reprisals would follow.

In an age of radical mass revolution, there was one kind of mutiny that sent a hush through the corridors of gentlemanly power. The spectre of a mass mutiny that would strip Britain of its defences in the name of republican, or even French republican, rule haunted the Navy and the propertied nation through the 1790s – and in 1797 it looked as if their direst predictions had come to pass.

For a time that summer almost every major warship in home waters flew the red flag of rebellion. For a few weeks the nation gazed into the abyss of life without a Navy, and politicians acted as if the whole service had been turned into traitors at the behest of a few particularly successful agitators.

This was the Navy's standard line on mass mutiny, useful in that it allowed for most offenders to be sent back to work with a flea in their ear. It also avoided any need to consider the underlying grievances that set off the cataclysm of 1797.

SPITHEAD

British seamen's main grievances were pay-related, most particularly their failure to receive a wage rise in 150 years. Petitions posted at sea in early 1797 were sent to the 'sailor's friend', retired Admiral Howe, but were ignored as the work of troublemakers. More petitions were delivered direct to the Admiralty and the parliamentary opposition when the Channel Fleet returned to Spithead in late March, and plans were made to seize the ships if they weren't answered.

Preparations were hardly secret, adding to the sense of a modern industrial dispute that surrounds the episode, but the Admiralty reacted to advance warning of the proposed mutiny by ordering the fleet to sea as a countermeasure. Announcement of the orders on 16 April, Easter Sunday, triggered the mutiny two days earlier than planned, and the fleet passed smoothly into the hands of two sailors' delegates from each ship.

While delegates drew up a detailed list of demands, discipline and order were maintained throughout the base, and mutineers repeatedly expressed their willingness to fight if needed. The mutiny ended on 24 April after the government agreed to address all grievances, but a final demand for more fresh food in port was not met, and ships were seized again from 5 May. This time the authorities moved quickly to appease the mutineers – Howe and delegates from the original mutiny toured the fleet appealing for trust, and the rapid passage of a new Sailors' Bill guaranteeing pay rises restored ships to their officers by 15 May.

A man killed amid violence on Admiral Colpoys' flagship was the only casualty at Spithead, and all the mutineers were pardoned. Copycat outbreaks meanwhile spread around the coasts. Most were orderly industrial disputes, resolved with similar restraint, but the mass uprising at the Thames Estuary base of the Nore was an altogether nastier business.

THE FLOATING REPUBLIC

Warships at the Nore were taken over by their crews on 20 May, but delegates displayed little of the discipline or intelligence that won the day at Spithead. Their leader was an unhappy former gentleman, Richard Parker, once an officer but gradually busted down to ordinary seaman, and apparently very bitter about it.

Self-styled 'President of The Floating Republic', Parker was a genuine public relations disaster. He allowed the mutiny to develop half-baked radical pretensions, and his regime was characterized by revenge attacks on unpopular officers. Wild behaviour on ship and ashore contributed to the mutineers' general unpopularity, as did their success in infecting the main North Sea base at Yarmouth, where Admiral Duncan was abandoned by all but two ships as he sailed to resume his blockade of the Dutch fleet.

Parker's dictatorial style soon made enemies among the steadier seamen at the Nore, and signs of crumbling solidarity persuaded the government to abandon negotiation. Instead it mobilized public fear of revolution with a vigorous propaganda campaign, passed a law making it treason to consort with mutineers and posted troops to cut their supply lines. As

Richard Parker, leader of the Nore mutiny in 1797, presents a list of seamen's demands. Parker's unbending attitude to negotiations, his sponsorship of revenge attacks on unpopular officers and his manifest delight in his own authority all contributed to his rapid downfall. So did the alarm aroused in establishment circles by his espousal of French revolutionary principals, a factor pointedly ignored in this illustration. (Hulton Getty)

if to confirm their power to ruin the land, the mutineers responded by closing the mouth of the Thames and seizing all traffic for a day in early June.

The rebellion fell apart after the Admiralty repeated an offer to pardon all but the ringleaders on 6 June, and finally collapsed with Parker's overthrow aboard the *Sandwich* on 15 June. Parker was hanged a fortnight later, and 411 other ringleaders were arrested, but 300 were pardoned and only 28 were executed. The Navy was anxious not to waste too many precious professionals.

A sailor's progress, as viewed by a Georgian satirist. Even as a figure of fun, the Navy's lowliest recruit was reckoned more than a match for a few undernourished Frenchmen. Less believably, he was also expected to survive into a relatively prosperous retirement, complete with the unlikely blessings of all four limbs and a Navy pension. (By George Cruikshank, Hulton Getty)

The Nore wasn't the end of mutiny in the wartime Navy – individual ships were apt to turn against tyrants well into the nineteenth century – but the incidence of large-scale uprising declined sharply after 1797. This was the great achievement of the Spithead mutineers, and of the Admiralty that eventually took them seriously. By winning substantial pay rises, improved food, an end to the purser's 'eighth' as well as better treatment for the sick and injured, the Channel Fleet delegates dragged the Navy into the age of modern labour relations, and made it a happier, more efficient service.

Entering as Landsmen —
Carousing on board —
In Irons for getting drunk —
Boarding a French brig —
Promoted to Boatswain & excercising his Authority —
Laid up a Greenwich pensioner — relating his adventures —

The SAILORS PROGRESS — sic transit gloria mundi —

DRINK

Though regulated rations of beer, wine and (watered) rum were undoubtedly good for morale, alcohol abuse was rampant at every level within the service and drink caused a great deal of trouble aboard ships. Officers and most NCOs could almost always find a way to get drunk on duty if they chose, while an ordinary sailor could hoard his grog rations and be found drunk at extraordinary times.

Drunks made mistakes, ignored discipline and got into fights. Either striking a superior officer or any kind of blow to the face was regarded as a serious offence, usually punishable by flogging, but cases of murder, mutiny and negligence were often the result of drunkenness, which has been cited as at least indirectly responsible for half the cases brought to court-martial during the period.

FLOGGING

The captain generally only delivered minor punishments on his own authority, condemning men to lashes by the dozen for any number of small offences. What exactly merited a flogging, which was carried out by

A flogging is about to begin aboard a man-of-war. Marines and, unusually, a drummer boy are drawn up on the quarterdeck, seamen crowd aft of the mainmast, and the officers watch from the left. The bosun stands ready with his cat-o'-nine-tails, and the prisoner is lashed to the frame for punishment … but the ritual is halted as another man confesses to the crime. (By George Cruikshank, Hulton Getty)

the bosun's department in front of the whole crew, varied wildly from captain to captain. Men accused of theft or drunken disobedience could expect the 'cat-o'-nine-tails', but some captains flogged men to punish them for simple inefficiency.

Flogging itself was regarded as a normal and acceptable form of punishment by crewmen, but outbreaks of muttering among the watchers would soon let officers know if they had punished the wrong man. An inconsistent captain risked crumbling morale and deep personal unpopularity, greatly increasing his vulnerability to mutiny.

An alternative punishment for thieves was known as 'running the gauntlet'. The guilty man would be given a dozen lashes and then dragged around the upper deck tied to a wheeled seat. All the crew would be armed with knotted ropes and required to cut the offender as he passed. To prevent leniency by shipmates, anyone noted failing to strike hard would be assumed guilty of the same offence, but it was the occasional deaths of unpopular crewmen that brought an end to the practice by Admiralty order in 1806.

COURTS-MARTIAL

Crimes meriting sentence of death, imprisonment, dismissal or more than about thirty lashes were tried by court-martial, as were serious accusations against officers by crews.

Usually held on board a ship, often in the great cabin of a flagship, a court-martial was a very imperfect instrument of justice. It consisted of between five and thirteen officers ranked captain or above, along with a secretary. That many captains could not often be got together, and many prisoners spent months on remand awaiting trial, usually in irons aboard ship.

Once in court, the defendant was permitted counsel, but this was unlikely to help most ratings or petty officers with complaints against superiors. Despite claims that the pace of proceedings, delayed while every statement was recorded in longhand and read back, gave an enterprising man plenty of time to concoct a defence on the spot, the great majority of verdicts went the way of officers. Officers on charges were judged by peers without legal training or guidelines, and their fate rested on a sympathetic hearing rather than any formal consideration of evidence.

Once a man had been found guilty, the penalty was usually laid down in the 36 Articles of War, which described in detail the crimes and punishments recognized by the Navy. Most of the Articles dealt with offences by officers, and twelve gave the court no choice but to execute or dismiss a guilty man. The remainder allowed limited discretion, but in general the members of a court were not required to be imaginative when it came to retribution.

A captured deserter unable to plead mitigating circumstances could expect three hundred lashes, delivered in batches, but punishments of up to a thousand strokes were not unknown for repeated offenders or mutineers. Anyone sentenced to more than a hundred might be 'flogged round the fleet' as an example. This involved being strapped to a frame aboard a rowing boat, and given a portion of the punishment in view of each ship at anchor. Alternatively, each ship would send a boat to witness the flogging.

The death penalty could be applied to men found guilty of, among other things, cowardice, treason, murder or sodomy, although the latter rarely came to court. Commissioned officers were usually executed by shooting, and hanging was generally good enough for everybody else. Naval hangings took place under the forward yard-arm of a ship, and were reckoned far more merciful than their land equivalents. The victim was hauled aloft by a party of sailors at high speed, and died almost instantly.

Whenever a warship was lost, the entire crew was automatically tried by court-martial. The majority were acquitted, and attention anyway focused on the commissioned officers and the captain, whose career could suffer from any censure handed down. If actually found guilty of a serious offence, a captain could expect at least demotion to the bottom of the seniority list, and possibly imprisonment for up to two years.

Though the Navy had stopped shooting senior officers as examples by the 1790s, commanding admirals were called to account when large-scale fleet operations went wrong, and especially if failure attracted public outcry. Admiral Calder was court-martialled after failing to attack the French and Spanish in July 1805, as was Admiral Gambier for his inability to finish off a French squadron in the Basque Roads four years later.

BRITONS STRIKE HOME – COMBAT

Sailors liked to sing. The men of Hornblower's Navy sang as they toiled, often bellowed lustily during Sunday services, and chorused bawdy shanties when at leisure. They also sang going into battle, and British fleets swept to many of their finest hours with the strains of 'Hearts of Oak', 'Rule Britannia' or 'Britons Strike Home' sounding above the wind and woodwork.

Though encouraged as good for morale, singing was an expression of high spirits rather than their catalyst. Combat was dangerous, but death was anyway a constant companion, and British crews were often more

Divine worship aboard Nelson's flagship Vanguard *after the Battle of the Nile in 1798. Only the most important vessels carried chaplains, and captains usually conducted religious services, often simply intoning the Articles of War by way of a lesson. Running to some four thousand words, and an exercise in linguistic pedantry, they could hardly have been understood by most of his audience. (By John Augustus Atkinson, The Bridgeman Art Library/The Stapleton Collection)* anxious for battle than their leaders. Their thirst for a fight stemmed partly from the boredom of peaceful patrolling, and partly from a faith in the Navy's combat superiority that reached down to touch even the humblest idler.

Victory was assumed, and might mean some small reward in prize money, but fighting was something sailors did for pleasure anyway, and many reacted to the prospect of killing or maiming Britain's enemies like the bloodthirsty xenophobes they were. Others more homesick or seriously inclined cited battle as the most tangible contribution they could make to ending the war quickly, but all displayed a delight in combat that was in marked contrast to the mood described aboard other European warships.

The quarterdeck of a 74-gunner cleared for action – a view highlighting the exposure suffered by commanders in battle. While crouching gun crews enjoyed at least the illusion of protection, the captain was required to stand upright on the quarterdeck. Though shielded from falling splinters by sauve-tête netting, and usually ringed by marines, he was a natural and relatively easy target for small-arms fire during any close-range combat. (National Maritime Museum)

Naval combat was essentially about ships fighting ships. Though warships fought against coastal forces, the contests were inevitably one-sided, with naval units enjoying a huge advantage over undefended targets but almost equally powerless against fortified shore artillery. Shore raids were land operations, and the main naval aspects consisted of getting men and sometimes artillery ashore, the latter one of the Navy's most impressive specialist tasks and one it performed to a standard that put most army gun crews to shame.

Once hostile warships came within sight of each other on the open sea, whether individually or in groups, the opening stage of a fight was usually the chase, as a ship bent on attack set off in headlong pursuit of a fleeing foe.

Sometimes darkness or fog would put enemies within firing range before they were aware of each other's presence, and well-matched single ships sometimes fought by mutual agreement, but the weaker party would usually run for its life. Foreign fleets almost always ran away from their Royal Navy equivalents, very sensibly regarding anything less than an overwhelming numerical advantage as insufficient protection against superior British techniques.

In small engagements the chase generally favoured the escapee, which was often smaller, lighter and faster, as well having the advantage of choosing its direction to suit the wind. But seamanship was also crucially important. A well-crewed and smartly rigged vessel could hope to overcome a faster but less efficient opponent, and as both unfurled sail to extract every inch of speed from the wind, one miscalculation by a captain could leave his ship dismasted and adrift.

Fleet actions were all about mass manoeuvre and position, with both parties capable of similar speeds. British forces were generally much better than their enemies at performing complex fleet 'evolutions' as they strove to cut enemy forces off from their coasts and get into attack range.

One of the most famous, if brief, single ship actions of the war period, the victory of the British frigate Shannon *over its US Navy counterpart* Chesapeake *in 1813 was one of several combats initiated with the agreement of both captains, who exchanged challenges before manoeuvring into attack positions. (Hulton Getty)*

Once a large vessel caught up with a smaller ship, the contest was effectively over. By convention, naval vessels avoided firing on ships of a smaller class unless absolutely necessary, and surrender of the weaker party usually followed. One broadside from a ship-of-the-line could virtually blow a frigate out of the water, and the same was true of a frigate's main armament turned against a little sloop. Frigates involved in fleet engagements were generally left alone by battleships provided they stuck to shooting at other frigates.

A full British gun crew in action. With seven men and a powder monkey around the weapon, the gun captain and loaders were able to work without pausing to haul it in or out. Any reduction in numbers, through casualties or crew shortfall, entailed a significant drop in rate of fire. (National Maritime Museum)

GUN WAR

As soon as adversaries of similar stature came within striking range, individually or as fleets, it was time for the singing to start.

The crew of a British warship would go to general quarters long before it came into gun range, and the decks would be cleared for action. The supply of roundshot always kept on deck would be topped up and augmented by boxes of grapeshot, and extraneous bulkheads would be knocked away to make room for the passage of 'powder monkeys', junior members of the gun crew equipped with covered containers to carry ready-made charges from the powder rooms to each gun. Gunpowder was never stored on deck during actions, and a screen was sometimes erected round the powder stores to act as additional protection against the spark that could blow a ship to pieces.

Gun crews were drawn from the ratings of the forecastle, tops, afterguard and waist, who each occupied a specific position when engaged in the duty. The biggest 32-pounder cannon were crewed by seven men each, and 18-pounders by six, but a ship was frequently only fighting with one broadside at a time, when the gun crews were doubled.

A gun captain for each weapon controlled elevation, priming and actual firing. He commanded one or two loaders, one or two men to bring them wads and shot, and a man to clean out the barrel, who joined any other crew in running the gun in and out. Gun crews were extremely stretched if both broadsides were in action simultaneously, but then the ship as a whole was probably in serious trouble anyway.

Unlike land artillery, which treated its work as an extension of mathematics, there was not a great deal of science about naval gunnery. The British did it better than their European rivals, but the secret of their success was an overwhelming concentration on rate of fire rather than accuracy. There was sense in this. Precision shooting was never really an option amid the pitch and yaw of a wooden ship racing towards its prey, and accuracy was hardly an issue in broadside contests conducted at close range.

DEATH GRIP – CLOSE-RANGE FIGHTING

Dominated by the elements, the tactics used to get in close for a fight were fairly simple. An attacker's aim was to achieve a position downwind of the opponent, preventing any rapid escape, before moving into close contact as quickly as possible against the wind. The means of reaching this position in fleet strength had been enshrined as the 'line of battle' orthodoxy, designed to limit the possibility of either side suffering annihilation.

Hostile fleets would each form a line ahead. The two battle lines would either pass in opposite directions, in which case the engagement would be brief unless both decided to turn round and renew it, or one would overtake the other, in which case the battle would develop as a number of essentially separate duels between individual or small groups of ships. An attacking fleet's approach manoeuvres, concerned with presenting a small target, would give way to combat manoeuvres at the closest possible range, as both parties attempted to bring broadsides to bear.

The Royal Navy's approach tactics underwent a significant transformation after 1796. As the only

PREVIOUS PAGE

The crew of the Shannon *boards the* Chesapeake. *Passing some forty yards behind his opponent, the* Shannon's *Captain Broke raked the* Chesapeake *with a highly effective broadside from a difficult angle, softening up its decks and superstructure for an immediate boarding operation. American captain Lawrence was killed during this attack, and the* Chesapeake *had surrendered within twenty minutes of the first cannon shot. (1816, aquatint by William Heath (1795–1840), The Bridgeman Art Library/The Stapleton Collection)*

OPPOSITE

Nelson's state funeral. The death of a lieutenant at sea was signalled by a volley of musket fire, and the loss of its captain put a ship in mourning, attracting salutes from all the warships in the area. Nelson's death at Trafalgar prompted one of the great pageants of Georgian Britain, and Forester placed his fictional hero in command of this massive flotilla on the Thames. (1806, coloured engraving by Joseph Mallord William Turner, The Bridgeman Art Library/Private Collection)

force without a vested interest in avoiding big naval battles, fleet attacks were turned into bids for total victory by a new generation of aggressive commanders. Admirals like Jervis, Duncan and Nelson, confident of their combat superiority, began launching attacks through enemy battle lines, approaching fast with the wind and risking destruction as they passed between hostile broadsides, before turning to pulverize their confused victims.

Unless a ship had already lost masts or been set ablaze by long-range shooting, a close-range gunnery duel would usually be decided by faster rate of fire. Most ships surrendered before they were sunk, captains preferring inevitable defeat to almost certain death in the water, but if neither hauled down its flag combat developed the characteristics of an infantry battle in miniature.

As ships became disabled and drifted helplessly together, the role of marines firing volleys of musket fire from the decks, and of sharpshooters in the rigging pouring light fire on to enemy decks, became more important. The action might ultimately be decided by boarding parties, still a very common way for single-ship engagements to end, with crews either swarming directly between ships locked together, or rowing to attack a disabled opponent.

The tough, experienced hands at the forecastle, armed with cutlasses and pistols, were generally reckoned the prime boarders on a British ship, and the topmen were the next to go over the side, brandishing pikes along with their pistols. Marines also joined boarding parties, which were usually led by lieutenants, though Nelson was by no means the only captain excitable enough to lead his storm troops in person.

The combination of aggressive approach work and dogged willingness to slug it out with heavily-armed but operationally inefficient enemies brought the Royal Navy an unprecedented run of success against hostile fleets in the eight years after the great mutinies, culminating in a victory at Trafalgar in 1805 that ended any prospect of a serious challenge to British fleet supremacy for another century.

BATTLE CASUALTIES

The Royal Navy lost less than five thousand men in all its major wartime fleet actions put together, compared with more than seventy thousand victims of disease, but this reflects the infrequency of battles rather than their mildness. A ship engaged in heavy close-range fighting was likely to lose anything up to 150 men in a day, and most of them would be likely to die horribly. The lucky ones were either killed instantly or saved by amputation, the only operation at which naval surgeons were generally at least competent. Complete lack of hygiene was likely to kill many of the wounded, with gangrene and blood poisoning, often from the gold braid on an officer's uniform, the standard causes of death.

PRIZE MONEY

In the aftermath of victory came the prize money. Having taken a warship, merchantman or privateer, and sent it to a friendly port under a skeleton 'prize crew', a captain was entitled to sell both prize and cargo to agents of the government. Most undamaged equipment and goods would be purchased, and the proceeds divided among the successful crew.

Until 1808, an eighth of the money went to the admiral commanding a successful ship's fleet and a quarter to the captain. An eighth was divided among the commissioned officers, ship's master and marine officers, an eighth among the warrant officers, an eighth among the midshipmen and petty officers, and the remaining quarter among the rest of the crew. After 1808, the admiral's share was reduced to a third of the captain's quarter, while the petty officers and ratings shared half the value between them.

Ships on detached duty paid no admiral's share, which went to the captain, and when more than one vessel took part in a capture, or was even within sight, all were deemed to deserve an equal share. The actual amount paid varied enormously according to the size, status and contents of a captured ship, and the expenses of the prize court that judged its value sometimes left little change.

Captains could become landed gentry overnight with one spectacular success, and admirals on lucrative stations (especially the pirate-infested West Indies) could expect to get rich. A rating with a sloop's relatively small crew might make six months wages from the capture of a well-stocked merchantman, or an intact vessel snatched by a 'cutting-out' operation, but the odds against making significant prize money below decks were very high indeed.

Great battle victories didn't tend to be very lucrative, since most of the ships captured had been smashed into near uselessness. Under these circumstances, though the system provided an incentive for aggression at sea and aided recruitment, it sometimes encouraged captains to avoid battle with warships in order to concentrate on prize-hunting.

Cutting out the French corvette La Chevrette. *Essentially the theft of an enemy ship in harbour — by sending a small raiding party into the anchorage at night, overpowering its crew and slipping away under cover of darkness — cutting out was both difficult and dangerous. If it worked it could also be very lucrative, delivering a prize undamaged by cannon fire. (By Philip James de Loutherbourg, The Bridgeman Art Library/City of Bristol Museum and Art Gallery)*

CHAPTER FIVE

A WORLD TO WIN: HORNBLOWER'S NAVY AT WAR

*B*ritain joined the first European coalition against republican France in February 1793. The two nations remained at war for more than twenty-two years, with only brief pauses during the ill-fated peace of 1802–03, and after Napoleon's first abdication in 1814. For the Royal Navy, which fought almost every other navy in the world at some time during the war years, this was the supreme test of its right to rule the waves.

DRIFTING IN

It was the French national assembly, high on revolution and conquest, that actually announced hostilities in 1793, but both sides had known war was coming since the previous autumn, when republican armies moved up to the Dutch frontier. British preparations for the fight had been in full swing since December, but any comparisons with grainy newsreels from 1939, or even 1914, should be forgotten. Away from the naval bases and dockyards, the nation mobilizing for war in 1793 was not something the average citizen was likely to notice.

The British government entered the fray half-heartedly, with no intention of becoming entangled in European land wars. It hired a few thousand German mercenaries to join Britain's tiny field army in Flanders, provided funds for Austrian, Prussian and Spanish armies to contest the French frontiers, and otherwise left it to the senior service.

Once it had been given time and money to bring hundreds of warships out of mothballs, the Navy could blockade the coasts of France, sweep up French colonies around the world, destroy French shipping, guard the world's trade routes, defend Britain and support a variety of long-range colonial adventures.

Samuel, Lord Hood, the admiral whose Mediterranean Fleet captured and then lost the French base at Toulon in 1793. The Hoods were one of Britain's great naval families, but both Samuel and his brother Alexander (who led the Channel Fleet as Lord Bridport) had seen their best days by the 1790s. Alexander's son, the younger Samuel Hood, later fought as one of Nelson's captains in the Mediterranean. (By James Northcote (1746–1831), The Bridgeman Art Library/National Maritime Museum, London)

These tall orders were to keep the Royal Navy stretched to the limit throughout the wars, and yet never quite provided a direct means of stopping French armies from conquering most of Europe.

FALSE DAWN – 1793–96

During the first few years of the struggle, lack of strategic focus was compounded by the Navy's own shortcomings. It entered the wars justifiably confident of its superiority over rivals, most whom were anyway ranged against France in 1793, but hidebound by tactics and leaders that belonged to an earlier generation.

Not that any weakness was immediately apparent. With only 25 ships-of-the-line in active service when the war started, the Navy was too busy building up to war strength to worry over-much about its operational efficiency. And by the late autumn, when there were 84 battleships in service all over the world, the defeat of France was starting to look a formality.

Preliminary skirmishes at sea seemed to confirm French naval weakness, and republican armies were retreating in Flanders. Meanwhile the French people seemed on the point of overthrowing their republican masters, and in August the veteran Lord Hood had shown the world what the mass deployment of sea power could achieve, leading his fleet into the Mediterranean and taking control of the main French naval base at Toulon. Meanwhile the Pitt government's global strategy seemed set fair for success, with Admiral Jervis and twelve battleships getting ready to extend Britannia's interests in the Caribbean.

But the false dawn soon passed, and it gradually became clear that the Navy wasn't winning the war.

Lax long-range blockades were allowing vital supply convoys into French ports, letting warships out to menace British trade, and failing to lure French fleets out to destruction. Old admirals like Hotham and Bridport (Hood's brother) were not the men to risk ships by pouncing aggressively at the first sign of a French sail, and several good opportunities went begging in the Mediterranean and the Atlantic.

Above all, the Navy was discovering that sea power alone, unless exercised with more efficiency and purpose, could do little to influence the great wars being fought on mainland Europe. Forces in the West and East Indies could seize minor colonies almost at will, but their successes were soon undermined by yellow fever and were totally overshadowed by the triumphs of French armies closer to home.

From late 1793, when a young Napoleon Bonaparte played an important part in recapturing Toulon with an overland attack, the French Army began transforming the political map of Europe. Within a year – while British forces marauded around the colonies and made hard work of capturing Corsica as a blockading base – they had pacified France and driven allied armies back from its frontiers.

Conquest and diplomacy brought the Dutch and Spanish fleets over to the French side during 1795, leaving Britain bereft of important naval allies and facing hostile forces all along the Channel coast. And in 1796, General Bonaparte announced his first independent command by conquering most of Italy and forcing the rest into French alliance.

Its duties still further extended by the need to blockade the Spanish and Dutch coasts, and forced out of its bases east of Gibraltar, the Royal Navy could only retreat from the Mediterranean altogether.

As new Mediterranean C-in-C Jervis sailed his outnumbered warships away to friendly Lisbon in December 1796, a French fleet evaded Bridport's Channel blockade to mount an invasion of Ireland at Bantry Bay, and its failure had more to do with the weather than the Channel Fleet. With its European alliances in ruins, and a French invasion army massing opposite the south coast, Britain suddenly woke up to the fact that an apparently unbroken stream of naval victories had led to the brink of strategic defeat.

THE GLORIOUS FIRST OF JUNE

On 1 June 1794, in the North Atlantic some 650km off the coast of Brittany, the Royal Navy won its only major fleet victory of the war's opening years. The British dubbed the day the 'Glorious First of June', revelling in what was an undoubted tactical success and pouring adulation on the victorious Admiral Howe, but that didn't prevent the French from celebrating the same battle as a strategic victory.

Admiral Villaret de Joyeuse, in command of the French fleet at Brest, was ordered to sea in spring 1794 to guarantee the safe passage of a vital food convoy of some 120 ships from the United States. At a time of near-famine in France, the convoy was more important than any number of men and ships, a strategic fact of life appreciated by the French but not by the Royal Navy.

Howe's long-range blockading force was far out in the Atlantic searching for the convoy when Villaret sailed with 26 ships-of-the-line on 16 May. Unable to locate his needle in a haystack, Howe eventually left nine battleships to comb the ocean, and got back to the coast on 19 May to find the French fleet missing. Faced with conflicting operational priorities, Howe went with tradition and devoted his energies to destruction of the enemy battle fleet. Ignoring the convoy, he set off in pursuit of Villaret.

Though Howe sighted the French fleet on 28 May, Villaret was one of the better seamen in a French high command decimated by the traumas of revolution. With help from fog, he succeeded in evading serious attack, keeping his ships together and drawing Howe away from the convoy for three days. Knowing that his under-manned and ill-prepared ships would have to fight sooner or later, to protect both the convoy and his own head, Villeneuve eventually accepted battle on the first morning of June.

The Mediterranean Fleet evacuates Toulon in December 1793. Forced to flee by artillery on the hills above the harbour, the British attempted to burn the French fleet as they departed. Despite the inferno raging in the background, the operation was only partly successful, leaving the French with 27 battleships worth repairing, and forcing the Royal Navy to maintain a full-scale blockade of the port. (1816, engraving by Thomas Whitcombe, The Bridgeman Art Library/The Stapleton Collection)

Howe's strategic performance may have belonged to the past, but his tactics hinted at glories to come. Ignoring orthodoxy, Howe flew flags that morning ordering his captains to approach the French battle line on a diagonal course from the windward side, pass through it and attack from the leeward side.

Only five battleships followed his flagship's instructions to the letter, others striking from the windward side or holding back altogether, but the attack was still devastatingly effective, throwing Villaret's line into rapid confusion and developing into separate mélées around isolated French ships.

Villaret's flagship, *Montagne*, led those ships not directly attacked to form a new line just downwind, but French battleships caught between British broadsides were overwhelmed. By the time firing stopped just before noon twelve French battleships had surrendered, although one sank a few hours later and five more eventually escaped to rejoin Villaret in heavy winds.

By then a completely exhausted Howe had handed direct command to his flag captain, and Villaret was allowed to take his battered force home without further interference. The British fleet then limped for home and the nation's applause with no further thought for the food convoy, which reached France completely unscathed.

Elderly and gout-ridden, Howe was content with his prizes and willing to allow Villaret an honourable withdrawal, an attitude in keeping with traditions of courtesy that would be totally alien to the next generation of British naval commanders.

CRISIS – 1797

Early 1797 found Britain alone at war against France, and the Navy with its back to the wall. During an action-packed year, when land warfare had all but ceased and Europe's attention was focused on naval affairs, the Navy fought back. In the middle of the year it survived the shock of great mutinies at Spithead and the Nore, emerging with restored vigour for the struggles to come. Either side of the summer, major victories over the Spanish and Dutch fleets at St Vincent and Camperdown demonstrated that much-needed operational reforms were well under way, and that aggressive commanders were emerging to lead the service to more complete successes.

The Battle of the First of June, 1794, a British victory marred by the unwillingness of several captains to enter the fight. Cowardice in the face of the enemy was a problem almost entirely restricted to senior officers. An exposed target on the quarter-deck, and the only man aboard with the leisure to contemplate danger or the authority to avoid it, the captain was uniquely vulnerable to bouts of discretion. (By Philip James de Loutherbourg, The Bridgeman Art Library/National Maritime Museum, London)

ST VINCENT AND CAMPERDOWN

The fearsome John Jervis, later Lord St Vincent, was perhaps the most important naval commander of the age, and was the most famous after Nelson. A brutal disciplinarian, and no respecter of social rank, he forged the Mediterranean Fleet into a fighting unit of unprecedented ferocity, was a reforming First Lord of the Admiralty from 1801 until 1806, and eventually became Admiral of the Fleet in 1821. (By William Beechey, National Maritime Museum)

The man principally responsible for raising the wartime Royal Navy to new standards of operational efficiency was John Jervis, iron disciplinarian and pragmatic fighting admiral. His four years in command of the Mediterranean Fleet from 1795 saw the introduction of new training and discipline regimes, along with the promotion on merit alone of exceptional captains like Nelson, Collingwood, Troubridge and Saumarez. By 1797 Jervis had turned the fleet into the most effective naval force the world had ever seen, and it announced its transformation against the unfortunate Spanish fleet of Admiral Cordova in February.

Jervis had only 15 battleships under his command off Cape St. Vincent when Cordova's 27 were sighted making for Brest from Carthagena on the morning of 14 February. The Spanish fleet had split into two loose groups during overnight mist, and was still reorganizing when the wind changed, giving the British an opportunity to dash through the gap between them. Jervis seized the chance without hesitation, ordering his captains into the charge at about eleven, and half an hour later the British line began exchanging broadsides with the larger Spanish squadron of nineteen battleships.

The two forces swept by each other, and both vanguards tried to turn once they reached clear water, but the Spanish turn was blocked by Nelson, commanding the 74-gun *Captain* three from the rear of the British line. Nelson pulled his ship out of line and into the path of the oncoming Spaniards, holding them off alone until the leading British ships came back up in support.

The outcome of the close-range gun duel that followed was never really in doubt. Nelson made his name legend by leading boarding parties to take both the *San Nicolas* and *San Josef* from the decks of the crippled *Captain*, and the battle died down shortly before four, when Cordova's 130-gun *Santissima Trinidad* hauled down its colours.

The *Santissima Trinidad* later escaped to join the isolated ships of the smaller Spanish division, and Jervis had to be content with four major prizes as survivors ran for Cadiz, but his sheer aggression in the face of heavy odds had reminded the world what an efficient Royal Navy might achieve.

Admiral Duncan's victory over the Dutch in October was even more comprehensive and equally important. Duncan's North Sea Fleet had been heavily affected by the Nore mutiny, and he was thirsting for an opportunity to test its morale in battle. The chance came in October, when Franco-Dutch authorities ordered Admiral de Winter's Dutch fleet to sea for a nuisance raid.

De Winter knew better than his masters how badly two years of confinement in port had affected his fleet. Though his sixteen ships-of-the-line got away from their base at the Texel while Duncan's fleet was re-supplying, he turned for home as soon as he heard the British had left Yarmouth. It was already too late, and sixteen British battleships were

The mélée at St Vincent. As British and Spanish battle lines merge for a climactic battle of attrition, Nelson's Captain *is locked in combat with two Spanish battleships. Nelson later led boarding parties that captured both Spanish ships. (By Thomas Luny (1759–1837), The Brideman Art Library/Christie's Images)*

OPPOSITE

Both Admiral Duncan (right) and his Dutch adversary, Admiral de Winter, were at the heart of the mélée at Camperdown, and both stood six feet four. By the time his flagship surrendered, de Winter was the only man unhurt on its quarterdeck. (1798, by Henri-Pierre Danloux (1753–1809), The Bridgeman Art Library/Scottish National Portrait Gallery, Edinburgh)

waiting when he reappeared off the Dutch coast on 11 October.

As soon as the Dutch fleet was sighted just off Camperdown, Duncan manoeuvred to get the wind behind his ships and sped towards his prey, determined to strike before it could escape into the coastal shallows. As de Winter formed a line and headed for the coast, looming only about ten miles away, Duncan threw away the rule book in favour of urgent attack, ordering his ships forward in a free-for-all that turned into something of a tactical masterstroke.

Largely by accident, the British men-of-war split into two divisions, outnumbering the rear and vanguard of de Winter's line, and leaving the centre with no one to fight. The mélée that followed had forced eight Dutch battleships to surrender by the time de Winter was compelled to give up his shattered flagship. Duncan allowed seven surviving ships to flee, but his unbridled thirst for a fight had ended any serious threat from the Dutch Navy and provided a tactical blueprint for the future.

Admiral Duncan's North Sea fleet abandons formal tactics and simply hurls itself at the Dutch fleet off Camperdown. Duncan led the attack by example.

OPPOSITE

Nelson's fleet overwhelms the French at the Nile. Two British ships, Goliath *and* Zealous, *have swung around the open end of the French line to attack its inner flank, and several of Nelson's captains have sliced through the line. (Both engravings circa 1830s, by Alexander Keith Johnston (1894–71), The Bridgeman Art Library/The Stapleton Collection)*

THE NELSON TOUCH

Discipline, aggression, speed, and now concentration of forces to overwhelm part of an enemy line ... the elements harnessed by Jervis and Duncan had not gone unnoticed by the man whose initiative had won the day at St Vincent, Horatio Nelson.

By the end of 1797, Nelson had become the Navy's most renowned man of action. His record as a Mediterranean captain was littered with successful single-ship actions, and he had won honour while losing an eye during the siege of Corsica. Promoted rear-admiral after St Vincent (at the cost of a few senior captain's careers), he lost an arm to amputation during a shambolic attack on Tenerife later in the year, but the dash and audacity of even that operation only added lustre to his reputation.

Passionate, excitable and prone to bursts of personal vainglory, Nelson was capable of folly on the grand scale, as his entanglement with Emma Hamilton and the lurid court intrigues of Naples were to demonstrate. But the sheer force of his personality eventually won over all who worked with him, and his ill-fitting features never lost their unique hold over the British popular imagination.

Nelson was genuinely adored by those who served under him, both officers and men. He brought an original genius to the art of naval warfare, combining an almost obsessive need to annihilate his country's enemies with an innate understanding of the tactical and psychological means to do so.

What he did best of all was win battles, and with none of Howe's gentlemanly satisfaction in a points victory. His first two crushing fleet victories, at the Nile in 1798 and at Copenhagen in 1801, opened and closed a period of strong recovery for the Royal Navy, when it reclaimed for itself the freedom of the seas.

THE NILE

While its allies were put firmly in their place, the French Navy made little effort to exploit its unaccustomed freedom of manoeuvre in the Mediterranean until summer 1798, when Napoleon's expedition to the Middle East forced Admiral Brueys to bring his warships out of Toulon as escorts. His thirteen battleships sailed for Egypt on 19 May, along with four frigates and about four hundred transports.

Both Jervis, now Lord St Vincent, and war minister Dundas believed that Egypt was Napoleon's destination, but dared not leave the routes to the Atlantic and Ireland unguarded until they were certain. Meanwhile Jervis could only spare Nelson with an élite task force of fourteen battleships and seven frigates to cover the eastern Mediterranean.

As Nelson sped to Alexandria, Napoleon stopped *en route* to capture Malta, so that the British fleet had gone off to Sicily for resupply by the time Brueys reached Egypt at the start of July. Ordered to remain at the mouth of the Nile and guard the rear of Napoleon's march on Cairo, Brueys anchored his ships in Aboukir Bay. Lining up his ships close inshore, their

BATTLE of THE NILE
1st August 1798.

guns ready for firing out to sea, Brueys thought he was ready when the British returned at the end of the month.

He reckoned without Nelson, who attacked as soon as he arrived, charging the vanguard and centre of the French line in the late afternoon of 1 August. Two of his ships found room to get between the coast and the front of the line, enabling them to attack the virtually unprotected French inner flank, and several more risked grounding to break through the gaps between Brueys' ships.

Heavy combat continued into the evening, but the French fleet was steadily destroyed in the crossfire, and Brueys was among those killed when his 120-gun flagship, *l'Orient*, blew up at about ten that night. Only two French battleships and two frigates eventually escaped to Malta.

The spectacular explosion that ended the Battle of the Nile at about ten o'clock on the night of 1 August 1798. French Admiral Brueys was one of almost a thousand killed when his flagship, the 120-gun l'Orient, *blew up, by which time British gun crews had reduced most of his fleet to wreckage. (By John Thomas Serres (1759–1825), The Bridgeman Art Library/Bonhams, London)*

It took a long time for news of the Nile to make its way to the capital cities of Europe, but its ultimate repercussions went far beyond the international renown it brought to Nelson. Russia, Turkey, Austria and Naples were all encouraged into a new coalition against France, and Napoleon found his army isolated in the Middle East as the Royal Navy took control over the Mediterranean.

SIDESHOWS –
THE SECOND COALITION

Success at the Nile proved a mixed blessing. Over the next three years a welter of additional responsibilities in the Mediterranean contributed to the Navy's continued failure to make a strategic impact on the land war. The captures of Malta and Spanish Minorca provided defensive headaches as well as good bases, as did a growing commitment to the defence of Sicily. Meanwhile a small French squadron at Alexandria needed watching, and warships were sent to undertake coastal operations against Napoleon's invasion of Syria in 1799.

With the government still committing naval forces to pointless and invariably unsuccessful military adventures all over Europe, and the acquisition of colonial real estate continuing apace, the Navy again found its strength dissipated. By the beginning of 1799 it could call on 192 ships-of-the-line, 25 old 50-gunners, 226 frigates and 345 sloops or similar vessels, but it could do nothing to prevent French armies once more sweeping into Italy and Germany.

By late 1800 the Second Coalition had all but gone the way of the first, and for a few weeks in early 1801, as Russia led the Baltic powers towards war against the 'tyrant of the seas', it looked as if the dark days of 1796 were about to return.

COPENHAGEN –
STING IN THE TAIL

Tsar Paul I of Russia, Catherine the Great's mad son and successor, was a man of extremes. When his alliance with the Second Coalition proved fruitless, he sprouted a powerful conviction that Britain was the source of all Europe's dismay. By the end of 1800 a combination of greed and fear had persuaded Denmark, Sweden and Prussia to join Russia in an Armed Neutrality League against Britain.

Ostensibly a joint stand against the Royal Navy's 'stop and search' blockade regulations, the League amounted to a bid to close the Baltic to British shipping. It was also a gamble, assuming that a war-weary British public would balk at the prospect of a fresh conflict so close to home.

In Britain, peace was in the air. With no sign of victory on the horizon, the new Addington government was expected to open negotiations with Napoleon's French regime, but the cabinet included Lord St Vincent as First Lord of the Admiralty, and he wanted naval supplies from the Baltic secured first.

As Armed Neutrality came into force during the opening months of 1801, the British government backed a diplomatic offensive with a fleet of 26 battleships, 7 frigates and 23 other craft. Its commander, the competent but cautious Vice-Admiral Hyde-Parker, was hardly the ideal man to throw the Navy's weight about, but Jervis made sure he got Nelson as second-in-command.

It took a while for the Nelson magic to work on the old man, who had become rich enough on the Jamaica station to have no need of glory – but the gleam in the eye got to him in the end, and Hyde-Parker eventually agreed to an extremely risky, two-pronged attack on the Danish fleet at anchor just outside Copenhagen.

Hyde-Parker led most of the fleet's heaviest ships towards the six Danish battleships guarding the northern approach to the harbour, but made little progress against wind and currents. Nelson meanwhile guided the twelve lightest ships-of-the-line through unmarked shallows to get into position beyond the main Danish battle line of fourteen battleships and several floating batteries, anchored in a narrow channel running southeast from Copenhagen12.

Nelson's ships inched into the attack on the morning of 2 April, and though three ran aground in the process, only one was too far way for its broadsides to be effective. While frigates were sent to keep the northern end of the Danish line distracted, a static gunnery duel developed around Nelson's flagship *Elephant* in the centre, where seven British ships took on ten Danish men-of-war and four floating batteries.

British gunnery was gradually overwhelming Danish defences by early afternoon, when Hyde-

Parker called off the battle in the belief that Nelson was losing. Nelson ignored his signal, ostentatiously reading it through his blind eye, and was backed by Admiral Graves at the rear of the line. Most Danish ships had ceased firing within another hour, though boarding parties met continued resistance until a truce was agreed that evening. With Copenhagen now under threat from an unopposed bombardment, the Danes agreed to break with the Armed Neutrality League and resupply their attackers.

The British fleet, now under Nelson's command, sailed off into the Baltic to deal with the Russians in early May, but the mad Tsar had been assassinated in late March, and his League was already dead. With Anglo-French talks now under way, Navy personnel the world over began making plans against peacetime unemployment.

This map of the Battle of Copenhagen, complete with an illustration of the final attack, gives a clear idea of why Nelson needed to manoeuvre into position behind the Danish line. It does no justice to the risks he ran to reach that position, edging his ships through treacherous, uncharted shallows, along channels stripped of marker buoys by the Danes. (Hulton Getty)

TRUCE – 1801–03

The Mediterranean Fleet enjoyed one more success in July 1801, when a Franco-Spanish squadron was severely mauled off Algeciras by Saumarez, before the peace of Amiens ended hostilities in October.

By the time the peace was finalized the following March, it was already starting to look very temporary. Britain had agreed to give back almost all its wartime conquests in return for promises of non-aggression from Napoleon, but he was already breaking them by moving to cement French control over northern Italy and the Netherlands.

Meanwhile an increasingly unpopular Addington government had little choice but to go through with the peacetime naval cutbacks it had promised. As more and more ships dropped out of commission, their precious crews paid off, the government's decision to hold on to Malta until Napoleon kept his promises set the clock ticking, and the process of mobilization began again when war resumed on 16 May 1803.

Despite the government's efforts, the Navy's overall situation was far better than it had been a decade before. Applying his talent for pragmatic reform to naval administration, Jervis had already put forty new 74-gunners under construction and begun an overdue standardization of gun design. Both measures encouraged a steady widening of the gap between the Navy and its declining rivals.

ENTER NAPOLEON

The new war began with a restoration of familiar patterns. Blockades were in place around the French-controlled European coasts within a few days, and colonial forces set about reclaiming their prizes. Nelson returned to the Mediterranean as C-in-C, and French forces were once more massed for a cross-Channel invasion. But there was also a new element at work in the naval war. French naval strategy, and to an extent that of its allies, was now under Napoleon's control. The campaign that brought the battle fleet war to a dramatic and premature end was triggered by Napoleon's peculiar military genius. Aware that he couldn't hope to get an invading army across the Channel while the Royal Navy blocked its path, he set in train an elaborate decoy operation from spring 1805.

French and Spanish fleets from the Atlantic and Mediterranean were to break through British blockades and speed for the West Indies, where they would meet up and turn straight for home. While the British were still lumbering in pursuit, a massive Franco-Spanish force would sweep into the Channel and escort Napoleon's invading armies to southern England.

The plan was a fantasy, treating half-crewed warships crowded with troops as if they were armies capable of precision long-range manoeuvre. Its northern component failed at the first hurdle, with Napoleon's ships remaining bottled up in port, and Admiral Villeneuve's successful escape from Toulon proved a very mixed blessing.

Slipping past Nelson's risky long-range blockade, Villeneuve gained a three-week head start after the British went searching for him in the eastern Mediterranean. By the time he had picked up Spanish forces from Cadiz, sailed the Combined Fleet to Martinique and returned to Europe, the lead was down to four days. His luck held out a little longer, as Nelson guessed wrong and turned south for Gibraltar, but any hope of actually attacking into the Channel disappeared when his move north was intercepted by Admiral Calder's blockading forces.

Though he was allowed to escape after a skirmish on 22 July, Villeneuve made little effort to resume the offensive, and took advantage of a loophole in Napoleon's latest set of attack orders to retire his battered, diseased ships into Cadiz in August.

Nelson had returned to England on leave when news of the Combined Fleet's flight to Cadiz reached London in early September. He left Portsmouth aboard HMS *Victory* on 14 September, and took command of blockading forces off Cadiz two weeks later. Napoleon had meanwhile abandoned invasion plans

NELSON

The son of a Norfolk village clergyman, Nelson was born in 1758 and joined the Navy at twelve. Though without social influence, his luminous talent brought rapid promotion, and he began the wars in command of the battleship *Agamemnon*, attached to the Mediterranean Fleet. His part in the capture of Corsica (where he lost an eye) and several single ship actions had already won him considerable renown before a brilliant performance at Cape St. Vincent in 1797 earned him a knighthood, promotion to rear admiral and popular adulation at home. An audacious, if ill-conceived, attempt to take Tenerife later that year did his reputation no harm, though it cost him an arm, and his demolition of the French fleet at the Nile in 1798 established him as Europe's most celebrated sea dog.

At this stage international hero-worship seems to have gone to the newly ennobled Lord Nelson's head, which had been wounded at the Nile. While recovering in Naples, he began a notorious affair with Emma Hamilton, wife of the British ambassador, and became deeply involved in the machinations of Europe's most corrupt court.

Once recalled to action in 1801, Nelson added unprecedented lustre to his name with a spectacular victory over the Danish fleet at Copenhagen that same year and the annihilation of Franco–Spanish sea power at Trafalgar in 1805. His death at Trafalgar was greeted with a display of national grief seldom matched before or since.

Horatio Nelson as a young officer. Nelson joined the Royal Navy as a boy of twelve and impressed every commander he served during early stints in the West Indies, the Arctic and the East Indies, and was commissioned lieutenant in 1777. Promoted post captain at twenty-one, he commanded a frigate under Samuel Hood in America from 1780, and was then stationed in the West Indies, where he married Frances Nisbet in 1787. The following year he took her home to Norfolk, where he lived on half pay until the outbreak of war against France. (By J. F. Rigaud, National Maritime Museum)

Nelson's death at Trafalgar quickly became the stuff of legend. Despite the inclusion of some interesting and accurate details, such as the presence of a woman in an unofficial nursing capacity (bottom left), this florid representation owes more to the artist's sense of pageant and composition than to reality. Nelson was shot by a sniper on the main deck of the Victory, *but was then carried below while the battle raged for another four hours. In this version, the physique and dress of crewmen, their battle positions, their unlikely combat roles as spectators or commentators, and even the* Victory's *basic structure, have all been warped to invest the demise of a great imperial hero with the trappings of classical tragedy. (By Daniel Maclise (1806–70), The Bridgeman Art Library/Walker Art Gallery, Liverpool, Board of Trustees: National Museums and Galleries on Merseyside)*

in the face of a third coalition, organized by Pitt since his return to power in 1804, and ordered Villeneuve to re-enter the Mediterranean with his entire force, carrying all available troops for a campaign in southern Italy.

Napoleon's orders also included the answer to Nelson's prayers. Exasperated by the realities of naval warfare, he insisted that the Combined Fleet seek to engage the enemy. Villeneuve was understandably horrified, but expected to be replaced if he argued, and led the Franco-Spanish fleet southwest with the first fair wind on 19 October.

TRAFALGAR – LAST BATTLE

The Combined Fleet included 33 battleships, six more than were available to Nelson, but nothing like enough to give it a realistic chance in battle. As he sailed south through that day and the next, Villeneuve expected to be attacked and defeated. Nelson was equally sure of victory, and kept his distance for two days solely to avoid frightening his prey back into Cadiz.

During the second night Nelson moved his ships in for the kill, and the two fleets were only about twelve miles apart by dawn on 21 October. As Villeneuve began to form a battle line, the British fleet manoeuvred into position to the west, forming two loose columns as it bore down ahead of a light northwesterly wind. Nelson in the *Victory* led eleven battleships towards the Franco-Spanish vanguard, and second-in-command Collingwood led fifteen towards the rear of the Combined line.

Like Duncan's ships at Camperdown, the Mediterranean Fleet wasted no time on keeping formation, but simply raced into action at top speed. As the columns approached, the Combined Fleet attempted to turn for Cadiz, but the clumsy manoeuvre achieved only confusion, leaving Villeneuve's line strung out in two loose divisions when the British ships struck.

Collingwood's *Royal Sovereign*, far ahead of the rest of his column, was first through the Combined line at around noon, and survived a few minutes against overwhelming odds before support arrived to grapple the sixteen ships of Spanish Admiral Alava's ragged rear division.

Meanwhile *Victory* and *Temeraire* led the group crashing into the rear half of Villeneuve's forward division. Nelson's *Victory* passed just astern of the Spanish *Santissima Trinidad* and Villeneuve's flagship *Bucentaure*,

Nelson, with Collingwood on his left, explains plans for the Battle of Trafalgar to the Mediterranean Fleet's captains. As an admiral from 1797, Nelson forged his captains into a 'band of brothers', taking great care to ensure that they understood his tactical plans well in advance and in detail. His trust was rewarded with an unprecedented level of commitment to hazardous enterprise. (Hulton Getty) before ramming the French *Redoutable*. Casualties mounted as crews fell to close-quarters fighting, but the gap created allowed more British ships to join in as the battle degenerated into the mêlée that Nelson had planned.

As the leading six Combined Fleet ships-of-the-line moved off unmolested, remaining vessels found themselves outgunned and outmanoeuvred in a chaos of gunfire, with regular arrivals of slower British ships steadily lengthening the odds against them. By about one-fifteen, when a sniper aboard the *Redoutable* shot and mortally wounded Nelson, the condition of hostile ships around *Victory* had degenerated almost beyond resistance.

Nelson died shortly before the last of eighteen Franco-Spanish ships to surrender hauled down its colours at around five in the evening. The remainder escaped, and although four ships from the unengaged vanguard made a brief attempt to intervene, they were chased off by the last two British ships to reach the scene.

Nelson's death left Collingwood in command, and he performed wonders to get his severely damaged ships safely home through a storm that struck next day and lasted for almost a week. One captured French ship escaped to Cadiz, and all but four of the other prizes were destroyed on the rocks, but the Royal Navy no longer needed to add to its collection of useless hulks.

Trafalgar ended any serious threat to the Navy from hostile battle fleets for the rest of the century. It also imposed permanent geographical and economic limits on French imperial expansion, putting Napoleon's confirmation as the master of European land warfare at Austerlitz into a global perspective.

AFTERMATH – THE SEARCH FOR STRATEGY

An era of great sea battles ended with Trafalgar, partly because every naval force that could hope to meet the Royal Navy on comparable terms had been eliminated. The war at sea went on for another ten years, but it was no longer a contest, rather a case of the British policing their secure domain and continuing to search for a strategic role in the land war.

It didn't prove easy. Fleet actions aside, the Navy's global responsibilities remained unchanged. Over the next five years, as Collingwood wore himself to death coping with the endless complexities of Mediterranean command, the unceasing vigils of blockade and patrol became steadily more arduous as Napoleon extended his empire.

Even when the Navy was able to attempt independent strategic intervention, its efforts remained marginal and unconvincing. Vice-Admiral Duckworth ruined his personal reputation as one of the Mediterranean Fleet's finest by sailing into the Dardanelles Straits in early 1807, failing to bully the Turkish government into an alliance and sailing away without firing a shot. Far to the north that autumn, a fleet was sent to dissuade the Danes from an alliance with France. It bombarded Copenhagen, killing two thousand civilians, and then it too sailed away, seizing the few surviving Danish Navy vessels but outraging European opinion and ensuring Denmark's bitter enmity for the next seven years.

One aspect of the otherwise unhappy Copenhagen affair pointed to the strategic future of sea power. Some thirty thousand troops had taken part in the raid, and standards of inter-service co-operation had shown a marked improvement. One of the generals involved was Arthur Wellesley, soon to win fame in Spain as Lord Wellington, and it was his long Peninsular campaign after 1808 that finally provided the Navy with a means to strike directly at the French land empire.

The Navy's ability to deliver troops, supplies or artillery attacks anywhere on the Portuguese or Spanish coasts was a vital factor enabling Wellington to achieve long-term success in the Peninsular War. It was a task the senior service evidently performed with great relish, despite its earlier problems working with the despised army, and the seizure of Santander as a forward supply base before the Vitoria campaign in 1813 was perhaps the most strategically important of all its operations after 1805.

stantly just over the horizon, Jervis was ready to pounce on anything entering or leaving. If for some reason his battleships were called away, the frigate patrols would remain, daring hostile shipping to risk an escape.

Close blockade work imposed an enormous strain on ships and crews required to spend months on station, often in conditions of extreme tedium, but it did provoke severe economic disruption and some regional hardship in France. It also fed Napoleon's determination to succeed with his own economic counter-offensive, the Continental System, a vain attempt to close European coastlines to British trade that warped French imperial strategy from its inception in 1806.

As part of its overall blockade policy, the wartime Navy claimed the right to stop and search any neutral vessel suspected of trading with an enemy, and to seize those caught breaking contraband rules of its own devising. Imposed on neutral shipping wherever it was encountered, British search and confiscation procedures were hardly more popular worldwide than Napoleon's craving for land conquest. International outrage at Britain's high-handed behaviour rose steadily after 1806, and a series of stop-and-search incidents were directly responsible for the outbreak of war against the United States in 1812.

BLOCKADE

For the first few years of the wars most British fleets had attempted to seal off coasts using the 'open blockade' system, keeping large warships far out to sea in the hope of intercepting slow merchant convoys, and of tempting hostile fleets into an ambush. The system had the advantage of allowing warships to make frequent trips home for rest and repair, but it hardly ever actually worked.

The Mediterranean fleet under Jervis operated much more successful 'close' blockades. By deploying fast frigates within sight of blockaded harbours, and keeping a number of ships-of-the-line posted con-

FUTURE SHOCK – THE WAR OF 1812

Just as the war in Europe began to turn decisively in Britain's favour, a small war in a faraway place gave the Royal Navy an unwelcome glimpse into the far distant future.

Provoked by British seizures of American merchant shipping, the Anglo-American War of 1812 was by and large a waste of time for all concerned. Small armies meandered indecisively around the Canadian frontier for two years, and the Navy imposed a highly effective coastal blockade, but a treaty in Europe had already ended the war as a draw when the British lost their only important land battle at New Orleans in early 1815. The one really interesting aspect of the struggle was the battle for local supremacy between British and US Navy light forces – a contest which, intriguingly, the Americans won hands down.

Powerful American frigates didn't have it all their own way on the high seas, but light forces on the Great Lakes consistently got the better of comparable British flotillas. Perry's victory on Lake Erie in 1813 was the most comprehensive and famous of several successes, and was won with a combination of good seamanship and tactical originality that would mark the US Navy's eventual ascent to world power status.

ABOVE

After the slaughter. This wistful evening fantasy groups Nelson's most famous ships – Captain, Foudroyant, Elephant *and* Victory *– all of them in considerably better condition than when he left them. They were the last of their kind: the next generation of British ships called to fight a major war would be steam-driven ironclads. (1807, by Nicholas Pocock (1741–1821), The Bridgeman Art Library/National Maritime Museum)*

OPPOSITE

Cuthbert Collingwood, Nelson's greatest friend and the Georgian Navy's forgotten hero. Collingwood performed brilliantly as second-in-command at Trafalgar, and then took over the Mediterranean Fleet. His administrative rigour and strategic insight were central to the Fleet's success in fulfilling its myriad commitments, but he was denied the battle that would have sealed his fame for posterity. (By Colvin Smith (1795–1875), The Bridgeman Art Library/Crown Estate/Institute of Directors, London)

SUNSET

American sea power would one day dominate the oceans, but in 1815 they were ruled by the Royal Navy as never before. It had taken on and beaten all potential rivals, helped break the greatest land empire Europe had ever seen, and extended its control to the four corners of the globe, shepherding British maritime trade to a position of overwhelming world dominance.

But as the men and ships of the Royal Navy stood down from a war footing in 1816, most were going home for the last time. Their success had set Britain on a path of almost unbroken peace and prosperity, and the Navy's next major war would be conducted by ironclad monsters with no fear of winds or tides.

Life at sea would be safer, altogether more uniform and less completely separate from the landsman's world. Enclosed bridges would replace quarterdecks, and with them would go powder monkeys, topmen and many of the exotic special skills that made a Georgian sailor a man apart. Britannia would still rule the waves for much of the new age, but the waves would be a little more tame, and the raucous, bloodstained glories of Jervis, Nelson and the great sailing Navy would already be relics of a lost past.

SELECT GLOSSARY OF CONTEMPORARY NAVAL TERMS

Abaft the rear of a ship or any position towards the rear

Abeam at right angles to a ship's length

Afore to the front of the ship, in front

Aft to the rear of the ship, behind (abbreviation of *after*)

Aloft high on the mast, yards or rigging

Amidships in the middle of the ship

Astern behind

Athwart across

Bar an area of shallow water in the mouth of a harbour or river

Barque three-masted ship with a distinctive mixed sail configuration

Barricade parapet running along either side of the open deck

Beam direction at right angles to the ship's length

Bear up, Bear away change course to run before the wind

Beat proceed against the wind by tacking

Belay tie up, secure

Bends the main timbers on a ship's sides

Bilges the bottom of the ship, usually containing waste water

Binnacle cabinet holding the compass, positioned in front of the wheel

Boarding nets nets extended from the side of a ship to prevent boarding

Boom spar that holds a fore-and-aft sail in position

Bowlines ropes tied to sails as a means of pulling them forward

Bowsprit small spar projecting from the front of a ship, used to hold the jibboom in position

Box haul to turn a ship sharply in a confined space

Brace rope attached to a yard for fixing its direction

Breeching the rope attached to a gun and the ship's side, preventing it from being run too far

Brig, Brigantine a two-masted, square-rigged ship

Bring to to turn a ship's bows into the wind and arrange its sails in contrary positions, bringing it to an almost complete halt

Bulkhead any partition inside a ship

Cable a heavy rope

Cable's length a measurement about 240 yards

Cable tier storage space for cables, on the orlop deck

Capstan an upright cylinder on a spindle, to which poles could be attached, that was used as a pulley to bring up heavy cables

Careen to lay a ship on its side, either beached or afloat, so that the hull can be cleaned

Cat to haul an anchor out of the water to the height of the forecastle

Cat-head the spar projecting from the forecastle on which a catted anchor was hung

Caulk to plug the gaps between a ship's planks by filling them with oakem and sealing it with pitch

Close-hauled condition of a ship rigged to sail as directly into the wind as possible

Club-hauling tacking by using an anchor

Coamings the rim of a hatchway protruding above the deck planks

Con to direct a ship by instructing the helmsman

Cordage rope and the materials used to make it

Courses the lower propulsion sails on a ship's fore and main masts

Crimp to somehow gain control over a seaman and sell him to a ship a man engaged in the trade

Cruiser any ship or group of ships on detached patrol duty

Cutter a small, single-masted vessel, usually less than 20 tons

Deckhead an on board ceiling

Driver a gaff sail attached to the mizzen mast of a ship

En flute the condition of a warship with some or all of its guns removed

Flag officer an admiral

Fore the front of a ship; forward

Forecastle short deck built over the forward part of the main deck

Gaff a yard supporting the top of a sail

Galliot a small oar-driven vessel

Gantline a rope passed through a block high on a mast, used for loading and other haulage

Gasket a plaited rope tie, holding the sails to the yards

Ground tackle anchors, cables and associated equipment

Halliards, Halyards ropes for raising and lowering sails

Haul off to move away

Haul the wind to close-haul a ship

Heads crew toilets

Heave to to bring a vessel to a halt into the wind; tighten the anchor cable prior to hauling it in.

Jib the triangular sail joined to the fore-mast and the jibboom

Jibboom the spar jutting from the prow of a ship

Larboard the left-hand side, now called port

Lateen sail a triangular sail

Leeward in the same direction as the wind

Loggerhead a tool for applying heated pitch

Log-line a piece of wood attached to a line and thrown overboard. The line was knotted at regular intervals, and allowed to pay out freely, so that the number of knots pulled overboard in a given time enabled calculation of the ship's speed

Luff to turn a ship closer to the direction of the wind

Lug sail an asymmetrical four-sided sail

Lying to, Lying by the condition of a ship having been brought to.

Mast a vertical spar holding sails, yards and gaffs.

Mizzen the rear section of a ship

Muster a ship's list of personnel; to enter someone on the list; the full crew; an assembly of the full crew

Ordinary an uncommissioned warship ship in dock i.e. paid for by the Navy's ordinary peacetime budget

Orlop deck a ship's lowest deck

Packet a small courier vessel

Pay off to decommission (a ship)

Pinnace a ship's boat

Plying turning to windward

Point high steer as close into the wind as possible

Poop deck a short deck structure above the rear of the quarterdeck

Private ship any warship not carrying an admiral

Quarterdeck a deck running above the rear half of the main deck, fulfilling the functions of a modern bridge

Ratlines ropes linking the shrouds, used as ladders

Reef to reduce the size of a sail by tying part of it to the yards

Royals square sails just beneath the topgallants

Run to desert

Run ashore a brief period of leave

Scantling any part or parts of the hull structure

Sheets control ropes attached to the lower corners of sails

Shoal a dangerously shallow stretch of water

Shrouds lateral support ropes attached permanently to the masts

Slings heavy ropes (and sometimes chains) supporting the yards from the masts

Slipping the cable cutting the anchor line (after attaching a marker buoy for recovery purposes)

Square-rigged rigged with square sails across the bow

Stays fore-and-aft support ropes permanently attached to the masts

Stern gallery an open gallery running the width of a large ship's stern, outside its commander's cabin

Studded sail, Stunsail a small lug sail attached to the edges of the mainsails

Sweep a large oar

Tack to turn a ship about by steering to windward, or to zig-zag as a means of making progress against the wind

Taffrail the rail running round a ship's stern

Top a platform built around the mast, serving as a working area for crewmen, and as an additional support for rigging ropes

Topgallant the highest of three wooden spars joined to make a mast, or a sail attached to it

Warp to to change a ship's course by pulling on ropes attached to a stationary object

Wear to turn a ship about by turning its prow to leeward

Weather to sail to windward of something

Weigh anchor to lift up the anchor

Windage the distance a strong wind blows a ship off course

Yard a horizontal spar across the mast, from which sails are suspended

Yardarm the outer extension of a yard

INDEX

Page numbers referring to illustrations are in *italic*

First published in 1998 by Orion Media
Orion House, 5 Upper St Martin's Lane, London WC2H 9EA

Copyright © Steve Pope 1998
The right of Steve Pope to be identified as the author of this work has been asserted
in accordance with the Copyright, Designs and Patents Act 1988.

All rights reserved. No part of this publication may be reproduced, stored
in a retrieval system, or transmitted, in any form or by any means,
electronic, mechanical, photocopying, recording or otherwise, without
the prior permission of the copyright owner.

Picture credits
page 2: *A Tribute to Nelson*, circa 1820, English school
(The Bridgeman Arts Library/Crane Kalman, London)
page 3: *Napoleon Bonaparte aboard HMS* Bellerophon *at Plymouth, 1815* by John James Chalon
(1788-1854) (The Bridgeman Arts Library/National Maritime Museum, London)
page 4: *The Battle of Dogger Bank, showing the* Holland *at the rear of the Dutch line with frigate*
Amphitrite *alongside,* 1781 by Engel Hoogerheyden (1740-1809) (The Bridgeman Art Library/Phillips,
The International Fine Art Auctioneers)

A CIP catalogue record for this book is available
from the British Library.

Printed and bound in Italy

'ENGLAND EXPECTS THAT EVERY MAN WILL DO HIS DUTY'

VICE-ADMIRAL LORD NELSON
TO THE MEDITERRANEAN FLEET, OCTOBER 1805

C.S. FORESTER'S GREAT FICTIONAL COMMANDER INHABITS A TIME OF REAL HEROES AND ADVENTURERS UNIQUE IN THE ILLUSTRIOUS HISTORY OF THE ROYAL NAVY. IN TWO DECADES OF ALMOST CONTINUOUS WARFARE AFTER 1793, NELSON'S WARSHIPS AND THEIR CREWS ACHIEVED A BLEND OF SKILL AND INSPIRATION THAT SWEPT ASIDE ALL RIVALS.

MOST OF THOSE ABOARD NELSON'S WARSHIPS WERE SOCIETY'S DREGS, MANY HAD BEEN VICTIMS OF VIOLENT KIDNAP, AND ALL SAILED IN CONDITIONS THAT WOULD SHAME A MEDIEVAL DUNGEON. WHAT ALCHEMY MADE SUCH MEN THE TRUSTED, ALMOST INVINCIBLE, GUARDIANS OF AN EMPIRE?

THIS BOOK TELLS THE EXTRAORDINARY TRUTH BEHIND THE DASH AND GLORY OF HORNBLOWER AND HIS TIMES.

WRITER AND HISTORIAN STEVE POPE IS A FORMER OXFORD SCHOLAR AND CO-FOUNDER OF THE DESIGN AND REFERENCE GROUP. HIS MAJOR HISTORICAL WORKS INCLUDE SUCCESSFUL ENCYCLOPEDIAS OF THE FIRST AND SECOND WORLD WARS, AND THE FORTHCOMING *Dictionary of the Napoleonic Wars* FOR WEIDENFELD & NICOLSON.

FRONT COVER: **The Battle of Cape St.Vincent, 1797** BY R.B. BEECHEY © PHILIPS THE INTERNATIONAL AUCTIONEERS/THE BRIDGEMAN ART LIBRARY
BACK COVER: DETAIL FROM **Portrait of Lord Nelson with Santa Cruz beyond** BY LEMUEL FRANCIS ABBOTT © BONHAMS, LONDON/THE BRIDGEMAN ART LIBRARY

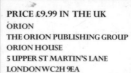

PRICE £9.99 IN THE UK
ORION
THE ORION PUBLISHING GROUP
ORION HOUSE
5 UPPER ST MARTIN'S LANE
LONDON WC2H 9EA

ISBN 0-75281-841-4

9 780752 818412

KT-806-193

Contents

Histograms and stem and leaf diagrams

Stem and leaf diagrams

A **stem and leaf** diagram uses the items of data themselves to provide a visual representation. The stem comprises the 'largest' part of the data item and the next digit appears as a leaf on a branch emerging from the stem. From such a display you can quickly gain an impression of the nature of the distribution of the data. Back-to-back diagrams are a valuable tool used in comparing two distributions.

Exam tips

You will not be asked to draw a stem and leaf diagram in the examination.

Fig. 1.1
a) a distribution of times.
b) a back-to-back comparison of heights of girls and boys.

a) Times

```
0 | 1  2  2  4  5  8  9
1 | 0  3  4  6  7
2 | 2  4
3 |
4 | 3
```

Key: 1|3 = 13 sec

b)

	Girls			13	Boys				
			4	13					
		9	8	14	4				
	8	7	5	15	6	9			
7	6	5	1	16	6	7	9		
	8	8	3	17	3	4	8	8	9
			6	18	4	6	7		
				19	0				

Key: 13|4 = 134 cm

All relevant branches will be shown, even those that do not have leaves on them. This is done in order to ensure the integrity of the display and any inferences drawn from it. A key reveals the magnitude (and nature) of the data. A diagram where the leaves are sorted according to size – often called 'ordered' – on each branch is useful.

Essential notes

The process of interpreting data from a stem and leaf diagram is called **juxtaposition**. A single leaf is placed alongside the stem.

Fig. 1.2
a) unordered
b) ordered

a)
```
2 | 3  5  4
3 | 8  6  2  4
4 | 0  5  1  7  6  9  2
5 | 3  9  4  8
6 | 2  1  5
```

b)
```
2 | 3  4  5
3 | 2  4  6  8
4 | 0  1  2  5  6  7  9
5 | 3  4  8  9
6 | 1  2  5
```

Key for (a) and (b): 2|3 = 23

Essential notes

Truncation is used to store data without rounding.

In the construction of a stem and leaf diagram, only the most significant (stem) and the next most significant (leaf) parts of each item of data are recorded. A leaf is only ever a single digit whereas the stem can be more than one digit. Any less significant digits are disregarded.

Example

The key to a stem and leaf diagram reads: '23|4 means 23 400 ml'. The item of data, 35 684 ml is to be included in the diagram.

a) On which branch from the stem would this item be recorded?

b) What leaf would be used to represent this item?

c) What is the maximum value that could be recorded on this branch?

Answer

a) The key shows that the stem holds the 'thousands' of ml. Hence the appropriate branch from the stem is the '35'.

b) Truncation rather than rounding is the process used to identify each leaf. This implies that the leaf is the next digit after '35' and no notice it taken of the '84'. The leaf will be '6'.

c) The largest volume on the '35' branch would have '9' as its leaf. This mean it would be 35 900 ml up to 35 999.99 ml. The maximum value could be almost 36 000 ml.

Histograms

A **histogram** is a means of displaying classified or grouped data. The total area of the display represents the number of items of data. In the same way, the area of each block represents the frequency of that particular class. The widths of the classes can – and usually do – vary. In this way the underlying characteristics of the data are appropriately and reliably conveyed.

For example, the hand spans of a class of children were recorded like this:

Hand span (cm)	Frequency	Class width	Frequency density
$12 \leq x < 15$	3	3	1
$15 \leq x < 17$	8	2	4
$17 \leq x < 18$	8	1	8
$18 \leq x < 19$	10	1	10
$19 \leq x < 21$	14	2	7
$21 \leq x < 24$	9	3	3
$24 \leq x < 28$	4	4	1

The classes are shown in the left hand column and the frequency is the number of instances within each one. The class width is based on the size of the class, and the frequency density is found by dividing the frequency by the class width.

> **Exam tips**
> You will not be asked to draw histograms in the examination.

> **Exam tips**
> It is essential to know how to calculate the widths of classes.

The histogram looks like this:

Fig. 1.3
A histogram of the hand spans in cm
of a group of 56 children

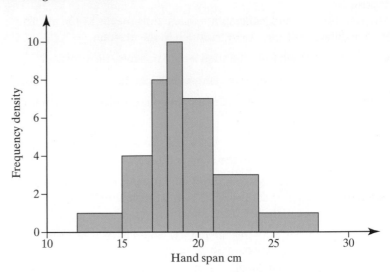

Essential notes

The horizontal axis records
the **data**. The vertical axis
records the **frequency
density**.

The histogram in Figure 1.3 shows that the children's hand spans are
approximately symmetrically distributed – in other words, there are
roughly the same number of children with small spans as there are with
large spans. There is a concentration of hand spans in the middle of the
range. The classes are narrower where there is a concentration of data and
wider where the data are more sparse. It could be argued that the data are
asymmetric rather than symmetrically distributed, and a definitive
response to this will be discussed later in the section on skewness.

Essential notes

Varying class widths enable
the detail to be revealed.

In this instance, the class widths are straightforwardly found from the
difference between the ends of each group just as presented in the table.
You will encounter other situations, for example where the data are ages or
where the measurements are rounded to the nearest major unit e.g. kg. A
mass recorded to the nearest kg as 14 kg could be as small as 13.5 kg or
nearly as large as 14.5 kg.

Essential notes

Always take into consideration
the nature of the data when
determining true class limits
to evaluate class widths.

Someone who records their age as 24 years will continue to do so right up
to the day before his or her 25th birthday. This means that a group shown
as, say, 21–24 years actually has a width of 4 years since the upper limit is
as close to 25 as possible and the lower limit is exactly 21. The same applies
when the data are counts, such as pensioners on buses. A class of 11–20 in
this case would have a width of 10 not nine.

Essential notes

The simplest approach to
determining frequency
density is to divide frequency
by class width.

In the hand span histogram, frequency density has been calculated by
dividing the frequency of each class by the width of the class. This means
that the label 'frequency density' really stands for 'frequency per cm'. This
method of dividing frequency by actual class width is often the easiest to
use, but it is not always employed. However, all methods require the
determination of the true class width.

Example

A frozen food company sampled its output of pizzas. The mass of each pizza was recorded to the nearest 10 g. Fifteen pizzas were in the 200–220 class. A histogram is constructed to display the results of the sampling.

a) What is the width of the 200–220 class?

b) What height is the block representing the 200–220 class if the vertical axis records

   i) 'frequency per g'?

   ii) 'frequency per 10 g'?

Answer

a) Since the mass is recorded to the nearest 10 g, the true class limits are given by $195 \leq x < 225$. This leads to the true class width being 30 g.

b) i) The frequency of the class is 15, hence the height of the block is $15 \div 30 = 0.5$ (frequency per g).

   ii) In the case where the frequency density is 'frequency per 10 g', the height of the block is $15 \div 3 = 5$ (frequency per 10 g).

Stop and think 1

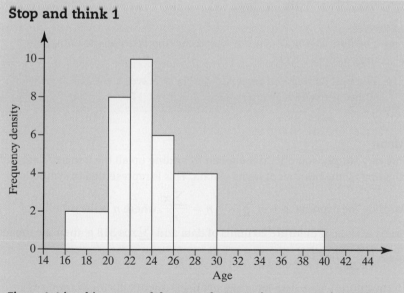

Fig. 1.4
Ages of 164 employees

Figure 1.4 is a histogram of the ages of 164 employees at an electronics company. How many employees are aged 26 to 29?

Measures of location

This section is about measures of location or, more simply, averages. These were introduced in GCSE: mode, mean, and median. The context of a problem is the deciding factor in which one to use.

Mode

The **mode** is the most frequently occurring item. This might be an actual item of data where these are available, or it might be a group or class.

Fig. 1.5
A stem and leaf diagram of heights.

Example

a) Identify the mode of the 21 heights recorded in the stem and leaf diagram.

b) What is the modal group as revealed by the diagram?

14	0	5						(2)
15	0	1	4	4	4	7		(6)
16	1	1	2	3	5	8	9 9	(8)
17	0	0	4	7				(4)
18	0							(0)

Key: 14|5 = 145 cm

Answer

a) The item 15|4 occurs more often than any other single item, hence the mode is 154 cm.

b) The branch with the greatest number of leaves is the '16' stem. Hence the modal group is $160 \leq \text{height} < 170$

Mean

Put very simply, you obtain the **mean** by adding up all the items of data and dividing by the number of items of data. This is represented in symbolic

Essential notes

You may sometimes see subscripts used to distinguish individual values, for

example $\bar{x} \approx \dfrac{\Sigma x_i f_i}{\Sigma f_i}$

form by the expression $\bar{x} = \Sigma x \div n = \dfrac{\Sigma x}{n}$, where n is the number of items of data. If there are 20 items of data and Σx is 318 g, then the mean mass is $\dfrac{318}{20}$ or 15.9 g.

In situations where data have already been classified – for example in a group frequency table – and you do not have the actual items of data, only an **estimate** of the mean can be calculated. Under these circumstances, the **mid-value** is chosen as x to represent each group and the mean is given by $\bar{x} \approx \dfrac{\Sigma xf}{\Sigma f}$ where f represents the frequency of each group.

Example

A sample of 66 commuters record their journey to work times (to the nearest minute) on one specified day. These times are presented in the table.

Time (minutes)	30–39	40–49	50–69	70–89	90–119
Frequency	8	14	23	12	9

Estimate the mean journey time.

Answer

The true class limits should be identified: the 30–39 class is strictly $29.5 \le x < 39.5$ (because the times were recorded to the nearest minute) and so on for the other classes. This leads to the mid-class values as representative x values:

x	34.5	44.5	59.5	79.5	104.5
f	8	14	23	12	9

The question tells you that $\Sigma f = 66$ and your calculator should show that $\Sigma xf = 4162$. This leads to $\bar{x} \approx \dfrac{4162}{66} = 63.06\ldots$ and so an estimate of the mean time is 63.1 minutes.

Exam tips

Make sure you take into account the precision of the data.

Table 1.1
Representative times.

Exam tips

There is no need to do the calculations by hand – use your calculator to the full.

Coding

It is sometimes convenient to transform data using a 'code' before calculating their means. This process can greatly simplify the subsequent calculations. For instance, the data in Table 1.1 might be transformed by subtracting 34.5 and then dividing by 5, $y = \dfrac{x - 34.5}{5}$, this would result in the following:

y	0	2	5	9	14
f	8	14	23	12	9

Then, $\bar{y} = \dfrac{\Sigma yf}{\Sigma f} = \dfrac{377}{66} \approx 5.712\ldots$, but this is the mean of the transformed data, so the estimate of the mean for the original data is obtained by reversing the transformation: $5.712\ldots \times 5 + 34.5 \approx 63.06$, just as before.

Essential notes

Skills and techniques learned in C1 may be needed in S1.

Essential notes

Recall how to solve an equation or rearrange a formula.

Essential notes

The position of the median is the $\frac{n+1}{2}$th item once the data are **ordered**

Median

This average is very readily understood – it is the middle value once all the data have been **put in order**. If there is an odd number of items of data, the median value will be an actual data item. Where there is an even number of items of data, the median is half-way between the two middle values.

Example

The number of hours of revision done by each of ten students in a specified week is shown below. Find the median time spent on revision.

10, 15, 9, 9.5, 0.5, 23, 8.5, 9, 12, 4.5

Answer

The data need to be ordered

0.5, 4.5, 8.5, 9, 9, 9.5, 10, 12, 15, 23

The median will now be the $\frac{10+1}{2}$th item of data. The 5th and 6th are 9 hrs and 9.5 hrs, so the $5\frac{1}{2}$th is $\frac{9+9.5}{2} = 9.25$ hrs.

Essential notes

Your calculator may be able to do this reliably.

Robustness

Consider the following data collection: 18, 20, 21, 22, 24. Both mean and median are equal to 21. What happens to these measures of location if it is realized that the item 18 had been wrongly recorded and should have been 13?

The median is not affected and it remains at 21. However, the mean is reduced to 20. The mean takes all values into account, and so a change in just one item of data can affect the value of the mean. On the other hand, the median takes into account just the middle of the data. The median is thus not affected by unusually large or small items of data. The median is known as a robust measure of location because it is not affected by extreme values.

Stem and leaf

Where data are presented in an ordered stem and leaf diagram much of the 'hard work' has already been done. Look at the data represented in Figure 1.5. There are 21 items and so the median is the 11th item. This will be represented by the third leaf along the branch with '16' as its stem. Hence the median height is 162 cm.

Grouped frequency

The concept of **cumulative frequency** is important when dealing with estimating the median for data presented in a grouped frequency form. Cumulative frequency, as the name suggests, is the total frequency up to (and including) the group with which it is associated. An appropriate **data value** needs to be chosen to be associated with each cumulative frequency.

In contrast to the case for the mean, the **upper class boundary** is used, because the cumulative frequency tells you the number of items that are less than or equal to this upper class boundary.

Exam tips

You need to **know** this – questions will not necessarily be explicit about using cumulative frequency.

Example

The time, in seconds, taken to complete five mental arithmetic tasks by each of 45 children is recorded in the table. Estimate the median time.

Time (s)	$10 \leq x < 30$	$30 \leq x < 40$	$40 \leq x < 45$	$45 \leq x < 50$	$50 \leq x < 90$
Frequency	8	9	10	7	11

Answer

Maximum time (s)	30	40	45	50	90
Cumulative Frequency	8	17	27	34	45

The median will be the $\frac{45 + 1}{2}$ th item, in other words the 23rd. From the cumulative frequency table you can see that the 23rd time lies in the 40–45 group. Since there are 17 times less than 40 seconds the 23rd will be the 6th time out of the 10 times in the group.

Estimating the median uses a process called **linear interpolation.** The class width is 5 seconds and so each of the ten values in this class will be at intervals of $\frac{5}{10}$ s. Therefore the median $\approx 40 + 6 \times \frac{5}{10} = 43$ s.

Essential notes

Accumulate the frequencies once you have identified the upper class values.

Linear interpolation uses proportionality. It assumes the 10 times in the group are **equally spaced.**

Large collections of data

Where Σf or n is large, it is perfectly acceptable to say that the location of the median is at the $\frac{n}{2}$ th position rather than $\frac{n + 1}{2}$ th. This is especially the case where the data are continuous.

Stop and think 2

The time taken for each of 60 cars to travel across a bridge is recorded in the table. The times were measured to the nearest second

Time (s)	0–19	20–29	30–39	40–49	50–59	60–89	90–119	120–299
Frequency	21	13	8	5	3	6	3	1

a) Obtain estimates of:

  i) The mean time;

  ii) The median time.

b) Explain why there is such a difference in these averages.

Essential notes

The difference between the maximum and minimum data values is called the **range**.

Measures of dispersion

Knowing about the **spread** or **dispersion** of data, in addition to knowing their average value, can be essential. Imagine the situation where there are two towns each of which has the same average annual temperature. In one town temperatures typically range from a minimum of 12 °C to a maximum of 20 °C. The minimum and maximum for the other town are −10 °C and 42 °C. Where would you prefer to live? The towns have the same mean but completely different ranges, so a measure of dispersion can be an important consideration.

Essential notes

Standard deviation
$= \sqrt{\text{variance}}$.

$$\text{Variance} = \frac{\Sigma(x - \bar{x})^2}{n}$$

Standard deviation

At this introductory level, the measure of spread associated with the mean is based on the average squared difference from the mean. The average squared difference is known as the **variance** and its square root is the **standard deviation**. Notice that if you did not find the square root you could have some unusual units, for example if the data are temperatures the variance could be in 'square degrees Celsius'.

Essential notes

$S_{xx} = \Sigma(x - \bar{x})^2$. Standard

deviation $= \sqrt{\dfrac{S_{xx}}{n}}$

Sum of squares

Later in the module, in the section on correlation and regression, you meet a quantity, S_{xx} called the '**sum of squares**'. It is at the heart of the standard deviation. The sum of squares is actually the **total of the squared differences from the mean**.

Essential notes

There is an alternative and often more convenient version of the sum of squares:

$$\Sigma(x - \bar{x})^2 \equiv \Sigma x^2 - \frac{(\Sigma x)^2}{n}$$

Example

The number of calls received at a call centre in 20 consecutive minutes was:

6, 1, 3, 4, 0, 4, 2, 3, 9, 4, 4, 3, 5, 0, 4, 6, 6, 4, 2, 5

Calculate the:

a) mean

b) sum of squares

c) standard deviation

Answer

a) $\Sigma x = 75$, so $\bar{x} = \dfrac{75}{20} = 3.75$

b) Sum of squares $= \Sigma x^2 - \dfrac{(\Sigma x)^2}{n} = 371 - \dfrac{75^2}{20} = 89.75$

c) Standard deviation $= \sqrt{\dfrac{89.75}{20}} = 2.12$

Note that the statistical functionality on some calculators will offer two possible values for the variance. Others may offer two possible values for the standard deviation. In either case, it is the smaller of the two offerings that you need in this module. In the above example, the other value a calculator gives for the standard deviation is 2.17.

Grouped frequency

Just as in the case of determining the mean, the formula for the sum of squares and hence standard deviation can be readily adapted to accommodate data given in grouped frequency format.

Exam tips

Make sure you know what information your calculator is giving you.

Essential notes

$$S_{xx} = \Sigma(x^2 f) - \frac{(\Sigma xf)^2}{\Sigma f}$$

Example

The length, in seconds, of the conversations resulting from the 20 calls in the previous example are summarized in the table below.

Time (s)	$0 \leq x < 20$	$20 \leq x < 60$	$60 \leq x < 120$	$120 \leq x < 240$	$240 \leq x < 600$
Frequency	8	2	5	3	2

Estimate the standard deviation of the times.

Answer

You need to use mid-interval values to represent each group:

10, 40, 90, 180, 420. Then you need to calculate the total time, Σxf, even though this is not explicitly sought.

$\Sigma xf = 10 \times 8 + 40 \times 2 + \ldots = 1990$

Sum of squares $= (10^2 \times 8 + 40^2 \times 2 + \ldots) - \dfrac{(1990)^2}{20} = 296{,}495$

and finally, the standard deviation $= 121.8$ seconds

Exam tips

Don't make the mistake of squaring the frequencies.

Advantages and disadvantages

The mean and standard deviation share the advantage that all items of data contribute to their evaluation. In this aspect they can be said to be representative of all the data. They are, however, adversely influenced by any substantially large or substantially small item(s) of data. They perform best when the data are symmetrically distributed. An alternative measure of dispersion which is suitable for asymmetric data is the **interquartile range**. This is based on quartiles.

Interquartile range

Quartiles

You have already met one of the **quartiles** – the second quartile which is more commonly called the median. For small collections of data, you need to identify the median before embarking on identifying the other quartiles. Q_1 (and Q_3) are the **middle items** of the lower (and upper) halves of the data **excluding the median**.

The interquartile range, IQR, is the difference, $Q_3 - Q_1$, between the third and first quartiles.

Essential notes

The quartiles are often denoted by Q_1, Q_2, Q_3 where $Q_2 =$ median

Method notes

Make sure the data are in order before starting.

This is a small collection of data, so you need to determine the median before embarking on the other quartiles.

Example

The number of orders a salesperson takes each week over a period of 13 weeks is: 5, 11, 13, 13, 14, 15, 16, 18, 19, 20, 21, 22, 22.

Determine the interquartile range.

Answer

Since there are 13 items of data, the median is the 7th (note that they are already in order). The 7th item is 16.

The lower quartile, Q_1, is the middle value of the first **six** items (5 to 15) hence it is between the two 13s, so: $Q_1 = 13$.

The upper quartile lies between 20 and 21, $Q_3 = 20.5$

Hence, IQR $= 20.5 - 13 = 7.5$

Essential notes

It is not possible to provide as convenient a description of the standard deviation.

Advantage

The interquartile range (sometimes called the quartile spread) measures the spread of the middle 50 per cent of the data. It has a tangible meaning. In common with the median, it is also unaffected by extreme values present in the data collection.

Stem and leaf diagram

The following ordered stem and leaf diagram contains 31 items of data. This implies that the median is the 16th item. Thus $Q_2 = 38$ cm.

```
2 | 0  2  3  4  6  8  9                    (7)
3 | 1  2  2  5  6  7  7  7  8  9  9       (11)
4 | 0  1  6  8  9                          (5)
5 | 2  4  4  5  6                          (5)
6 | 3  4                                   (2)
7 | 9                                      (1)
```

Key: 7|9 = 79 cm

Notice that 38 is the 16th item whether you start counting in the conventional way from the smallest item, 20, and getting larger, or starting at the largest item, 79, and getting smaller.

To identify Q_1 and Q_3, you exclude 38 cm leaving 15 items in each 'half' (20 to 37 and 39 to 79). So the lower and upper quartiles are 8th in their respective 'half': 31 cm and 52 cm.

This gives IQR $= Q_3 - Q_1, = 21$ cm

Essential notes

The cumulative frequencies of Q_1 and Q_3 are $\frac{n}{4}$ and $\frac{3n}{4}$ where $n = \Sigma f$

Group frequency

Where data have been grouped you will never obtain precise summary measures. To obtain estimates of the quartiles, the most sensible approach is to use cumulative frequency and associate this with the maximum class values.

Example

The lengths, to the nearest cm, of 60 standing jumps are recorded in the table. Obtain an estimate of the interquartile range.

Jump (cm)	20–59	60–79	80–89	90–99	100–109	110–129	130–149
Frequency	8	11	9	10	8	9	5

Answer

The lengths are recorded to the nearest cm, so the maximum lengths in the classes are 59.5, 79.5, etc. These are associated with the cumulative frequencies (C.F.) as shown below.

Upper class value, x	59.5	79.5	89.5	99.5	109.5	129.5	149.5
C.F.	8	19	28	38	46	55	60

The C.F. of Q_1 is $\dfrac{60}{4}$ the 15th value. This lies in the 60–79 class. Using linear interpolation: $Q_1 \approx 59.5 + 7 \times \dfrac{20}{11} \approx 72.2$ cm

Q_3 is the 45th value, hence $Q_3 \approx 99.5 + 7 \times \dfrac{10}{8} \approx 108.3$ cm

The interquartile range is $108.3 - 72.2 = 36.1$ cm

Exam tips

It is a useful approach to show the information you are planning to use in answering the question.

Exam tips

You could have used a cumulative frequency graph since the question does not demand the use of linear interpolation.

Skewness, outliers and box plots

The mean and standard deviation are suitable summary measures when data are approximately symmetrically distributed. In this situation the mean and median will either be equal or very nearly equal. In addition the median will be the same 'distance' from the lower and upper quartiles, that is $Q_2 - Q_1 \approx Q_3 - Q_2$.

Skewness

Where data are not symmetrically distributed, they are said to be **skewed**. Figure 1.6 shows histograms of two skewed distributions.

a)

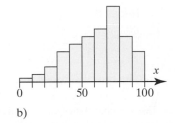

b)

Fig. 1.6
(a) positive skew
(b) negative skew

Essential notes

Note that 'Mean – Median' is alphabetic.

There are several measures of skewness. The simplest of these provides a direct indication of the nature of the skew. The sign of $(\bar{x} - Q_2)$ indicates the sign (positive or negative) of skew present in the data. Clearly, the magnitude of this will depend on the units used. Suppose the data were distances recorded in cm, then the value of $(\bar{x} - Q_2)$ would be one hundred times greater than the value calculated if they were measured in m. So this is a fairly crude measure of skewness.

The statistician, Pearson, whom you meet later, in the Correlation and Regression chapter, overcame the issue of units with his standard deviation based measure of skewness: $\dfrac{3(\bar{x} - Q_2)}{\text{standard deviation}}$

Exam tips

You do not need to memorize either of these. You will be told which to use if you are expected to calculate a specific measure of skewness.

A further measure of skewness avoids the use of the mean altogether. It relies entirely on quartiles: $\dfrac{(Q_3 - Q_2) - (Q_2 - Q_1)}{Q_3 - Q_1}$ (again its sign indicates the nature of the skew in the data.)

Exam tips

In an examination, you will be provided with the appropriate formulae to use

Example

The masses, xg, of a collection of 15 rocks have the following statistics.

$\Sigma x = 3787$, $\Sigma x^2 = 957093$, $Q_1 = 248$ g, $Q_2 = 252$ g, $Q_3 = 257$ g

a) Calculate:

   i) Pearson's measure of skewness;

   ii) The quartile based measure of skewness.

b) Comment on the nature of the underlying data distribution.

Answer

a) i) Pearson's measure of skewness needs the mean, median and standard deviation. Here,

$$\text{mean, } \bar{x} = \frac{3787}{15} \approx 252.5, \quad S_{xx} = \left(957093 - \frac{(3787)^2}{15}\right)$$

$$\text{and standard deviation} = \sqrt{\left(\frac{S_{xx}}{15}\right)} \approx 8.17\ldots$$

Hence Pearson's measure is

$$\frac{3(252.46\ldots - 252)}{8.71\ldots} = 0.171$$

Exam tips

Make full use of calculator values in subsequent evaluations.

   ii) The quartile-based measure is $\dfrac{(Q_3 - Q_2) - (Q_2 - Q_1)}{Q_3 - Q_1} \approx 0.111$

b) Both measures of skewness are positive and quite small, hence it is reasonable to conclude that the data are slightly positively skewed.

Outliers

An **outlier** is any item of data in a collection which is substantially larger or smaller than the majority of other items of data. There are a number of ways of identifying outliers. A common method makes use of the quartiles. Any item which is more than one-and-half quartile spreads ($1.5 \times$ IQR) above Q_3 or below Q_1 can be considered to be an outlier. An outlier is therefore any item x where $x > Q_3 + 1.5(Q_3 - Q_1)$ or $x < Q_1 - 1.5(Q_3 - Q_1)$.

Essential notes

There may be just one outlier or more than one. Outliers can be at either (or both) extremes of the data.

Example

Refer to the example in the skewness section above. Additional information informs you that the two extremes of the data collection are 238 g and 274 g. Is there evidence of any outliers in the data?

Answer

An outlier will be any item x where $x > Q_3 + 1.5(Q_3 - Q_1)$

or $x < Q_1 - 1.5(Q_3 - Q_1)$. This suggests that outliers will be such that $x > 270.5$ g or $x < 234.5$ g. Hence there is at least one outlier, 274 g.

An alternative method of identifying outliers uses the mean and standard deviation pairing. This identifies outliers as being **more than two standard deviations away from the mean.** In the above example it would suggest that if $x > 252.46 \ldots + 2 \times 8.17 \approx 268.8$ or $x < 236.1$. The same conclusion has been reached, but the quartile-based definition is somewhat more conservative.

Exam tips

Any other rules to identify outliers will be stated in an examination.

Box plots

A **box plot** is a powerful graphical way of displaying data in such a fashion that the essential features of the data and any outliers are immediately apparent. The information you need to have to hand is the **five-number summary** (the two extremes, the upper and lower quartiles and the median form the five numbers) together with the outlier boundaries (using the quartile-based definition)

Example

The 15 rocks mentioned in summary in the previous two examples have the following masses in g:

238, 242, 246, 248, 249, 250, 252, 252, 252, 253, 254, 257, 259, 261, 274.

a) Determine the five-number summary.

b) Are there outliers in the data?

c) Draw a box plot of the data.

Answer

a) The five-number summary is 238, 248, 252, 257, 274

b) Outliers are any items greater than 270.5 or less than 234.5

c)

Fig. 1.7
Box plot of the rocks

Essential notes

Where there is an outlier the 'whisker' goes only to the last non-outlier in the data.

The upper and lower quartiles determine the box and the median is shown within the box. The presence of the large outlier is made quite distinctly apparent in this box plot. Notice that 261 is the largest item of data which is not an outlier. This is where the upper whisker ends. There is no small outlier.

Stop and think 3

The stem and leaf diagram shows the marks gained in a test by 19 students in year 7.

0	3								(1)
1	8								(1)
2	4	7							(2)
3	3	8	9	9					(4)
4	2	3	3	4	6	8	9	9	(8)
5	0	0	0						(3)

Key: 1|8 = 18 marks

a) *Determine the median and quartiles of the data.*

b) *An outlier is defined as any item of data that is more than 1.5 quartile spreads away from the nearer quartile. Identify any outliers in the data, and illustrate the data in a box plot.*

Stop and think answers

Answer 1

Quite clearly the answer cannot be read directly from the vertical axis since this records the frequency density, not simply frequency. The area of the graph is proportional to the frequency. The total area is the sum of areas of all the bars, which is $4 \times 2 + 2 \times 8 + \ldots + 10 \times 1$ which comes to 82. But the total frequency is 164. So the constant of proportionality is 2.

Thus the number of employees aged 26 to 29 is 32 (the area is 4×4 multiplied by the constant of proportionality 2).

Method notes

The true width of the 26 to 29 year olds is 4. It appears as the block 26–30 in the histogram

Answer 2

a) i) $\bar{x} \approx \dfrac{\Sigma xf}{\Sigma f} = \dfrac{2155.25}{60} \approx 35.92\ldots, \approx 35.9$ s

Method notes

For the mean: mid values are 9.75, 24.5, 34.5, … 209.5

ii) *It is reasonable to consider that 60 items is a large collection.*

Time (s)	19.5	29.5	39.5	49.5	59.5	89.5	119.5	299.5
C.F.	21	34	42	47	50	56	59	60

Method notes

Upper class values are used.

Cumulative frequency of the median is taken as 30.

hence, the median $\approx 19.5 + 9 \times \dfrac{10}{13} \approx 26.4$ s

b) *More than half of the times are less than 30 s but there is a substantial minority that are more than twice this value.*

Answer 3

a) Median $= 43$, $Q_3 = 49$, $Q_1 = 33$

b) *The only outlier is the mark of 3.*

Method notes

Median is the 10th item and each quartile is 5th from either end.

Fig. 1.8
Box plot of the marks

Method notes

Outliers are

$> 49 + 1.5 \times 16$

or $< 33 - 1.5 \times 16$

Elementary probability and sample spaces

A weather forecast might read 'rain in the Southwest is probable before dawn but in the rest of the country there is only a possibility of it before sunset'. Here, the forecaster is trying to indicate that there is a high likelihood of rain in the Southwest and very little likelihood of rain elsewhere. In everyday speech, the terms 'probable' and 'possible' or 'probability' and 'possibility' are often taken to indicate degrees of likelihood.

In mathematics, the word '**probability**' is reserved exclusively for the **measure of likelihood** and the word '**possibility**' refers to an **outcome** or a situation which could occur.

An **event** is a collection of outcomes, the probability that a particular event occurs may be denoted by: P(event).

Mathematical models

A frequently invoked concept in elementary probability is that of '**equal likelihood**'. In this, each outcome is assumed to have the same probability of occurring so that the total of all the probabilities comes to 1 (representing certainty). The rationale for this model may be based on symmetry or on randomness.

Bags of coloured but otherwise identical beads, shuffled playing cards and so on rely on randomness to determine probabilities of individual outcomes. Unbiased dice with various numbers of faces, various numbers of flipped coins and so on invoke symmetry as the starting point of determining probabilities.

Sample space

A **sample space** diagram can be a useful way of deciding on the probability of an event. In a situation where all the equally likely outcomes are identified, summing those for the event produces the probability of that event.

Essential notes

Probability, P, is a number:
$0 \leq P \leq 1$

Essential notes

An unbiased octahedral die has eight faces. The probability associated with any given face being selected is $\frac{1}{8}$

Essential notes

You meet an alternative approach using a tree diagram later in the chapter.

Example

A bag contains three balls – red, green, and black – identical apart from their colour. An unbiased octahedral die has its faces numbered 1 to 8.

A ball is taken at random from the bag and the die is rolled. The number uppermost when the die comes to rest is noted. What is the probability of the event that the black ball is selected and the die shows a square number?

Answer

The equally likely outcomes are shown in the sample space (the table below) of 24 equally likely outcomes

Number Colour	1	2	3	4	5	6	7	8
Red	*	*	*	*	*	*	*	*
Green	*	*	*	*	*	*	*	*
Black	✓	*	*	✓	*	*	*	*

Ticks have been used to highlight the outcomes associated with the event.

The probability of the event is $\frac{2}{24}$ or $\frac{1}{12}$

Complementary events, mutual exclusion, conditionality

Two events are **complementary** if together they represent all possibilities and they have no common outcome. For example if three coins are flipped, then the events 'no head appears' and 'at least one head appears' are complementary. The probability of 'no head' is $\frac{1}{8}$, hence the probability of 'at least one head' is $1 - \frac{1}{8} = \frac{7}{8}$.

If A denotes an event, then A' denotes its complement. In the language used with sets, the intersection of A and A' is empty, in other words $A \cap A' = \varnothing$ and their union is the universal set, namely $A \cup A' = \xi$.

Two events are **mutually exclusive** when they have no outcome in common. This means that complementary events are mutually exclusive. However, mutually exclusive events are not necessarily complementary. Since mutually exclusive events have no common outcome, $P(A \cap B) = 0$ when A, B are exclusive.

Essential notes

$P(A') = 1 - P(A)$

Exam tips

It can be simpler to calculate the probability of the complementary event, then use the '$1 - P(A')$' result.

Essential notes

You need to know that if events A, B are mutually exclusive then $P(A \cup B) = P(A) + P(B)$

Essential notes

Recall that $A \cap B$ means the only region common to both A and B, and that $A \cup B$ means the whole of A together with the whole of B

Example

An ordinary pack of 52 playing cards contains 13 cards of each of four suits: hearts; diamonds; clubs; spades. Hearts and diamonds are red, and spades and clubs are black. A pack is shuffled and the top card is turned over. Three events are defined: A – the card is red; B – the card is a heart; C – the card is a spade. Determine the probability of each of the following pairs of events and state whether or not the pair are mutually exclusive:

a) A and B

b) B and C

c) C and A

Answer

a) $P(A \cap B) = P(\text{red and heart}) = \frac{1}{4}$, not exclusive.

b) $P(B \cap C) = P(\text{heart and spade}) = 0$, mutually exclusive.

c) $P(C \cap A) = P(\text{spade and red}) = 0$, mutually exclusive.

Conditional Probability

This is a 'first look' at **conditional probability**. It will be met again in the section on tree diagrams. Consider the situation where I shuffle a pack of 52 playing cards then, I ask 'What is the probability that the top card is a heart?' You correctly say $\frac{1}{4}$. This is the **unconditional probability** of a card being a heart. Suppose instead, I decide to look at the card myself without letting you see it. I now tell you it is red and ask you what is the probability that it is a heart. Since you know that the card is red, the probability that it is a heart is $\frac{1}{2}$. In fact, this is the conditional probability of a heart, given that the card is red.

Notice how this is not the same as unconditional probability. In notation form: $P(\text{heart} \mid \text{red}) = \frac{1}{2} \neq P(\text{heart})$.

Essential notes

You need to know the notation $P(A \mid B)$, for the conditional probability of event A given event B.

Example
What is $P(\text{red} \mid \text{heart})$?

Answer
Since all hearts are red, $P(\text{red} \mid \text{heart}) = 1$

Example
At the end of the year, 150 employees of a bank were interviewed about their pay. Some received a large bonus, others received a small bonus and 29 received no bonus. The table records this information according to whether the employee worked in the Investment division or elsewhere.

	No bonus	Small bonus	Large bonus
Investment	24	38	53
Elsewhere	5	28	2

One employee is selected at random. Let A be the event that the employee works in the Investment division and let B be the event that the employee receives a large bonus. Calculate:

a) $P(A)$

b) $P(A \cap B)$

c) $P(A \mid B)$

d) $P(B \mid A)$

Answer
a) There are 115 employees in the Investment division, hence
$$P(A) = \frac{115}{150}$$

b) 53 employees are both in the Investment division and received a large bonus, $P(A \cap B) = \frac{53}{150}$

c) The probability of the employee being in the Investment division given that they received a large bonus, $P(A \mid B)$, is $\frac{53}{55}$

d) The probability of an Investment division employee receiving a large bonus, $P(B \mid A) = \frac{53}{115}$

Exam tips

It is advisable to leave probabilities in fractional form rather than using a decimal approximation.

Statistical independence

You will often meet the concept of **independence** in the study of statistics and probability. This is a mathematical concept which is based on probabilities. If you are asked to justify the independence of two events, it is important that you stick to the mathematical definition – given in the Essential Notes. Do not be tempted to engage in discussions about the occurrence or otherwise of one event and its impact on the likelihood of another event.

Essential notes

Events A and B are independent if $P(A \cap B) = P(A) \times P(B)$

Example

In a box of chocolates the probability of a chocolate being soft-centred is 0.25, and the probability that the chocolate is coated in Belgian chocolate is 0.4. A chocolate lover observes that 15% of chocolates are soft-centred and coated in Belgian chocolate. Are the events: 'soft-centred', 'coated in Belgian chocolate' independent?

Answer

Let event A be 'chocolate is soft-centred', and event B be 'chocolate is coated in Belgian chocolate'. Then $(A \cap B)$ is the event that the chocolate is soft-centred and coated in Belgian chocolate. The information supplied gives $P(A \cap B) = 0.15$. But $P(A) \times P(B) = 0.25 \times 0.4 = 0.1$. Hence the events are not independent.

Alternative

An alternative mathematical relationship can be inferred from the consequences of independence. This equates the conditional probability of event A given event B, to the unconditional probability of event A. In other words, an alternative to the multiplicative relationship is $P(A|B) = P(A)$, equally $P(B|A) = P(B)$ when events A and B are independent.

Exam tips

You should learn the mathematical conditions for two events to be independent.

Example

An ordinary pack of 52 playing cards is shuffled and a single card is selected at random. The event C is that the card is a club. The event K is that the card is a King. Describe in words the following event $(K|C)$ and determine if C and K are independent.

Answer

The event $(K|C)$ is that the card is a king given that it is a club. There are 13 clubs and one of them is a king, hence $P(K|C) = \frac{1}{13}$. In a pack, 4 of the 52 cards are kings hence $P(K) = \frac{4}{52} = \frac{1}{13}$. So, $P(K|C) = \frac{1}{13} = P(K)$ which means that C and K are independent.

Exam tips

It would be equally correct to present the argument: $P(K) = \frac{4}{52}, P(C) = \frac{1}{4},$ and $P(K) \times P(C) = \frac{4}{52} \times \frac{1}{4} = \frac{1}{52}$ $P(C \cap K) = \frac{1}{52}$

The concept of independence can be extended to three or more events. For example, if events A, B, C are independent then:

$$P(A \cap B \cap C) = P(A) \times P(B) \times P(C)$$

Venn diagrams and tree diagrams

A **Venn diagram** shows the relationship between events and the numbers of outcomes in the various sub-events. For instance, suppose the relationship between two events A, B is given in the table:

Event	Number of elements
$A \cap B'$	7
$A \cap B$	5
$A' \cap B$	9
$(A \cup B)'$	23

The same information displayed in a Venn diagram would appear as shown in Figure 2.1

Fig. 2.1
The equivalent Venn diagram

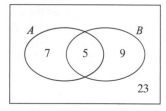

Example
With reference to the Venn diagram above, calculate:

a) Calculate

    i) $P(A)$

    ii) $P(A|B)$

    iii) $P(A \cup B)$

b) Determine if A and B are independent or mutually exclusive.

Method notes

It is clear from the Venn diagram that there is a total of 44 equally likely elements.

Answer

a) i) $P(A) = \dfrac{12}{44}$

    ii) $P(A|B) = \dfrac{5}{14}$

    iii) $P(A \cup B) = \dfrac{7+5+9}{44} = \dfrac{21}{44}$

Essential notes

The condition restricts interest to elements of B.

b) $P(A|B) \neq P(A)$ the events are not independent, and

    $P(A \cap B) = \dfrac{5}{44} \neq 0$ therefore A and B are not mutually exclusive.

Two **universal results** can be inferred from a general Venn diagram of two events. Consider generalizing the specific numbers of equally likely outcomes shown in Figure 2.2.

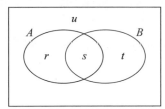

Fig. 2.2
A general Venn diagram

Then $n(A) = r + s$, $n(B) = s + t$, and $n(A \cup B) = r + s + t$ hence $n(A \cup B) = (r + s) + (s + t) - s = n(A) + n(B) - n(A \cap B)$ which translates into the **universal addition rule:**

$$P(A \cup B) = P(A) + P(B) - P(A \cap B)$$

A **universal multiplication rule** emerges from consideration of conditional probabilities: $P(A\,|\,B) = \dfrac{s}{s + t} = \dfrac{n(A \cap B)}{n(B)}$

Dividing both numerator and denominator by the total number of outcomes then gives:

$$P(A\,|\,B) = \frac{P(A \cap B)}{P(B)} \text{ or } P(A \cap B) = P(A\,|\,B) \times P(B)$$

Exam tips

The two universal rules are provided in the formulae book.

Essential notes

Equally conditionality may be reversed
$$P(A \cap B) = P(B\,|\,A) \times P(A)$$

Example

A teacher conducts a survey among a class of 30 students. She discovers that:

16	**Like the music of band A**
12	**Like the music of band B**
11	**Like the music of band C**
7	**Like the music of bands A and B**
6	**Like the music of bands B and C**
8	**Like the music of bands C and A**
5	**Like the music of all three bands**

a) Draw a Venn diagram to illustrate this information.

b) Find the probability that a student chosen at random does not like the music of any of the three bands.

c) Write down the probability that a student chosen at random likes the music of bands A and B, and, given that the student likes the music of band A find the probability that the student likes the music of band B.

☞ Continued on the next page

d) Find the probability that the student likes the music of band A or band B (or both).

e) Given that a student likes at least one band, find the probability they like the music of band B.

Answer

a)

Fig. 2.3
Venn diagram for events *A, B, C*

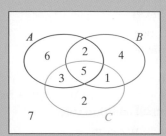

The place to start the Venn diagram is in the middle with the number of students who like all three – 5. Next, the numbers who like just two bands but not a third. Then those who like only one band and finally the number who do not like the music of any of the three bands. Hence the completed diagram shown above.

b) P(don't like any band) $= \dfrac{7}{30}$

c) The event 'likes A and B' is the same as $A \cap B$. The information supplied implies that $P(A \cap B) = \dfrac{7}{30}$

The conditional probability 'likes B given likes A' is

$$P(B|A) = \frac{P(A \cap B)}{P(A)} = \frac{\frac{7}{30}}{\frac{16}{30}} = \frac{7}{16}$$

d) The event 'likes A or B (or both)' is the same as $A \cup B$ so
$$P(A \cup B) = P(A) + P(B) - P(A \cap B) = \frac{16}{30} + \frac{12}{30} - \frac{7}{30} = \frac{7}{10}$$

e) The Venn diagram indicates there are 23 who like at least one band, of these 12 like band B hence the conditional probability is $\dfrac{12}{23}$.

Tree diagrams
A **tree diagram** is a valuable way of organizing your thinking when there is a clear sequence of events. It is particularly straightforward when the options at each stage are binary, that is, two mutually exclusive outcomes. When there are more than two options or more than two stages, care is needed.

Example

A farmer produces both organic vegetables and those on which fertilizer is used. The latter accounts for 65% of the produce. Root vegetables account for 25% of the fertilized produce and 45% of the organic produce.

a) Illustrate this information in a tree diagram.

b) Find what proportion of the farmer's produce are root vegetables.

c) A customer buys some root vegetables, what is the probability they were organically grown?

Answer

a) There are two stages and two options at each stage

b) Root vegetables can either be organic and root or fertilized and root, hence:

$$P(O \cap R) = P(O) \times P(R|O) = 0.35 \times 0.45 = 0.1575$$
$$\text{and} \quad P(F \cap R) = P(F) \times P(R|F) = 0.65 \times 0.25 = 0.1625$$

Therefore, the proportion of the produce that is 'root' is

0.1575 + 0.1625 or 32%.

c) This is asking you to find the conditional probability:

$$P(O|R) = \frac{P(O \cap R)}{P(R)} = \frac{P(O \cap R)}{P(R|O) \times P(R) + P(R|F) \times P(R)} = \frac{0.1575}{0.32}$$

$$\approx 0.492$$

Exam tips

When there is a lot of information use a tree diagram even if you are not told to do so.

Fig. 2.4
The farmer's tree diagram

Essential notes

In the second stage the probabilities are conditional.

Essential notes

You multiply along the branches and sum the results at the end.

Exam tips

Recall that the conditional probability formula is given in the formulae book.

In the above example, the tree diagram has the probabilities written on the branches and the events at the ends of the branches, this ordering may be reversed. Not all probabilities are essential provided there are sufficient for the reader to determine any that remain to be supplied. Where there are pairs of branches, the events must be complementary – a check on the relevant probabilities is worth making.

Essential notes

The probabilities of complementary events sum to one.

Stop and think

The tree diagram in Figure 2.5 shows two stages each with an event and its complement. Complete the diagram, then using the information find:

i) P(B')

ii) *The probability of A given B'*

Fig. 2.5
An incomplete tree diagram.

Stop and think answer

Fig. 2.6
A completed tree diagram.

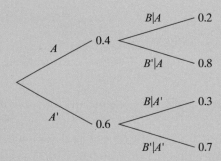

Method notes

$$P(A|B') = \frac{P(B' \cap A)}{P(B')}$$

i) $P(B') = P(B' \cap A) + P(B' \cap A') = 0.4 \times 0.8 + 0.6 \times 0.7 = 0.74$

ii) $\dfrac{0.32}{0.74} = \dfrac{32}{74}$

Scattergraphs and correlation

This chapter is about **bivariate data** – pairs of variables which are linked in some fashion. In essence the data that this section focuses upon are collections of points with coordinates: (x_1,y_1), (x_2,y_2), (x_3,y_3), ... Such a collection might be the blood pressure measurements of a group of patients at a local surgery. Blood pressure is always given as a pair of readings: the systolic and the diastolic pressures. Another collection might be the height and shoe size of students in year 12.

Scattergraph

Using the pairs of values of bivariate data as coordinates gives a graph which can be used to provide a visual indication of any underlying potential relationship between the two variables. The table below records the systolic and diastolic blood pressures in millimetres of mercury (mmHg) for eight patients.

Systolic, x mmHg	104	123	146	120	165	192	126	132
Diastolic, y mmHg	73	84	96	86	100	104	95	90

A graph of these data is shown in Figure 3.1

Fig. 3.1
Systolic vs diastolic blood pressure

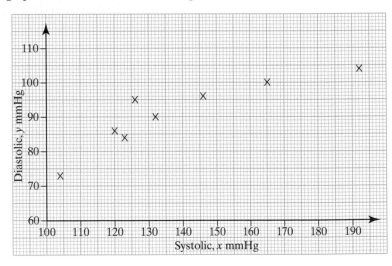

An interpretation of the **relationship** revealed in the scattergraph might be that it is **positive** – namely that larger values of one of the blood pressures corresponds to larger values of the other blood pressure. There are many possibilities in terms of the relationship between variables. Can you describe the relationship between the pairs of variables in each of the scattergraphs in Figures 3.2 to 3.4?

Exam tips

You may be called upon to plot data points on a graph – recall how to do this from your GCSE studies.

Exam tips

It is advisable to make reference to the **context** in which a question is set when making a comment.

Scattergraphs and correlation

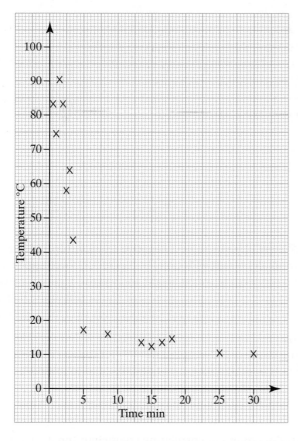

Fig. 3.2
Temperature (°C) of tea and
time (min)

Fig. 3.3
Height (m) of people and their
weight (kg)

Fig. 3.4
Height (m) of a ball and time (s)

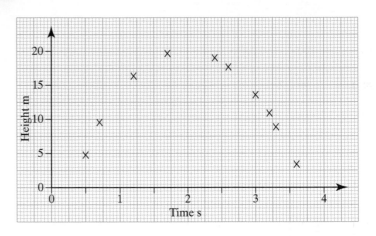

In Figure 3.2 there appears to be a **negative** relationship, in other words, the temperature decreases with time. In Figure 3.3, there appears to be little or no relationship between height and weight. Figure 3.4 suggests that there is a quadratic relationship, given that the height of the ball above the ground initially increases and then subsequently decreases, with time.

Correlation

A straight line is one of the simplest **models** for the relationship between two variables. It is straightforward to describe and to understand. Pearson, the statistician you met in connection with skewness, introduced a **correlation coefficient** as a measure of the strength of a **linear relationship**.

Pearson's **product moment correlation coefficient** (pmcc) has two particularly useful properties. Its **sign** is an indicator of the **nature** of the linear relationship between the variables. Its **magnitude** is an indicator of the **strength** of a linear relationship.

A positive value suggests that larger values of one variable correspond to larger values of the other variable. A negative value for the pmcc indicates that larger values of one variable correspond to smaller values of the other variable.

Pearson's correlation coefficient is bounded, its magnitude is never greater than one: $-1 \leq \text{pmcc} \leq +1$. The closer its magnitude is to one, the more likely it is that the relationship between the two variables is linear. In reality the value of $(\text{pmcc})^2$ tells you how much of the variability in the data can be attributed to linearity.

Derivation of PMCC

Consider the two scattergraphs shown in Figure 3.5. In your opinion does either show a positive relationship? Does either of them show a linear relationship? Which one shows the more positive linear relationship?

Essential notes

Linearity and straight line relationship essentially mean the same thing.

Essential notes

The letter r is used to denote the pmcc for a sample of data.

Exam tips

You are not required to memorize the use of r^2.

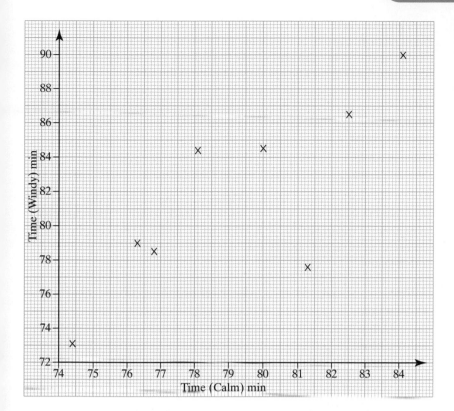

Fig. 3.5 a) Actual times
Race times (mins) in windy and calm conditions

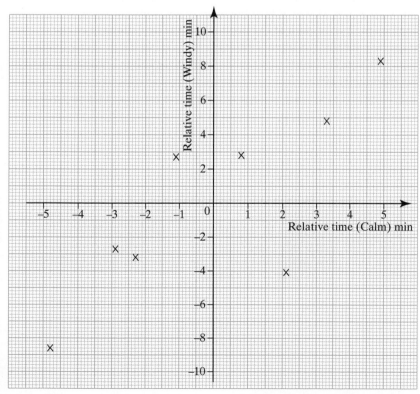

Fig. 3.5 b) Relative times
Race times (mins) in windy and calm conditions

Both graphs reveal a positive, possibly linear relationship. The data in each graph relate to a group of 8 athletes and their times for running a particular course in calm and windy conditions. The data for the scattergraph in Figure 3.5a are shown below in the table.

Essential notes

Use your calculator to confirm that $\bar{x} = 79.2$ and $\bar{y} = 81.7$

Athlete	A	B	C	D	E	F	G	H
Time in calm weather, x min	74.4	76.9	80.0	76.3	82.5	84.1	81.3	78.1
Time in windy weather, y min	73.1	78.5	84.5	79.0	86.5	90.0	77.6	84.4

To find the relative times shown in Figure 3.5b, the 'calm weather' times are related to their mean, $(x_i - \bar{x})$, and the 'windy weather' times are given an equivalent treatment, $(y_i - \bar{y})$. With the exception of the coordinates representing athletes G and H, the coordinates are either both positive or both negative.

Athlete	A	B	C	D	E	F	G	H
Relative calm, $(x_i - \bar{x})$ min	−4.8	−2.3	+0.8	−2.9	+3.3	+4.9	+2.1	−1.1
Relative windy, $(y_i - \bar{y})$ min	−8.6	−3.2	+2.8	−2.7	+4.8	+8.3	−4.1	+2.7

This implies that most of the products, $(x_i - \bar{x})(y_i - \bar{y})$, for the athletes will provide a positive outcome.

The sum $\Sigma (x_i - \bar{x})(y_i - \bar{y})$ is at the heart of Pearson's correlation coefficient. It is the **sum of the products of the deviations** from the respective means. It is often shortened to S_{xy}. It has the property that its sign indicates the nature of an underlying relationship. Calculating this for the above data gives:

Essential notes

You met S_{xx}, the sum of squared deviation from the mean, in connection with variance in Chapter 1.

$$\Sigma (x_i - \bar{x})(y_i - \bar{y}) = -4.8 \times -8.6 + -2.3 \times -3.2 + \ldots + -1.1 \times 2.7$$
$$= 103.64.$$

However, it suffers from being highly influenced by the units in use. If this was calculated in seconds it would be $-288 \times -516 + -138 \times -192 + \ldots + -66 \times +162 = 373\,104$. Clearly, a substantially larger number.

Pearson's product moment correlation coefficient overcomes this unit dependency by 'standardizing the variables'. This process is equivalent to dividing the relative times by their respective standard deviations. This sounds rather long winded and complicated, but there are convenient shortcuts available! In this first look at the product moment correlation coefficient, the shortcut gives the following:

$$r = \frac{\Sigma (x_i - \bar{x})(y_i - \bar{y})}{\sqrt{\Sigma (x_i - \bar{x})^2}\sqrt{\Sigma (y_i - \bar{y})^2}} = \frac{S_{xy}}{\sqrt{S_{xx}}\sqrt{S_{yy}}}.$$

Here the various summations are:

$\Sigma(x_i - \bar{x})(y_i - \bar{y}) = 103.64$, $\Sigma(x_i - \bar{x})^2 = 77.9$, $\Sigma(y_i - \bar{y})^2 = 215.36$

hence the pmcc is:

$$r = \frac{103.64}{\sqrt{77.9}\sqrt{215.36}} \approx 0.800\ldots$$

The product moment correlation coefficient is independent of the units used. This means you could convert the times from minutes into seconds in this example or, say °F into °C in a different context, before calculation and still obtain the same value for 'r'.

Interpretation

A value such as 0.800 (found above) for r is an indicator of a positive relationship between the calm and windy weather times. Quicker calm weather times correspond to quicker windy weather times, and there is a similar correspondence for longer race times.

An alternative method

There are many potential pitfalls in employing the form of r derived above. Fewer opportunities for error result if you use the original data together with their sums, products, and squares. The alternative formulation using

these summations is: $r = \dfrac{\Sigma xy - \dfrac{\Sigma x \Sigma y}{n}}{\sqrt{\left(\Sigma x^2 - \dfrac{(\Sigma x)^2}{n}\right)}\sqrt{\left(\Sigma y^2 - \dfrac{(\Sigma y)^2}{n}\right)}}$.

The following six 'sums' are needed before proceeding to calculate the product moment correlation coefficient:

$n = 8$ $\qquad \Sigma x = 633.6 \qquad \Sigma y = 653.6$

$\Sigma xy = 51\,868.76 \qquad \Sigma x^2 = 50\,259.02 \qquad \Sigma y^2 = 53\,614.48$

Putting these together in this alternative form yields:

$$r = \frac{51\,868.76 - \dfrac{(633.6) \times (653.6)}{8}}{\sqrt{\left(50\,259.02 - \dfrac{(633.6)^2}{8}\right)}\sqrt{\left(53\,614.48 - \dfrac{(653.6)^2}{8}\right)}} \approx 0.800 \ldots \text{ as before.}$$

Exam tips

Does your calculator allow you to input data pairs to obtain the value of r?

Essential notes

You may recall from Chapter 1 using :

$S_{xx} = \sqrt{\left(\Sigma x^2 - \dfrac{(\Sigma x)^2}{n}\right)}$ in place

of $\sqrt{\Sigma(x_i - \bar{x})^2}$

Exam tips

The various forms for the pmcc are given in the formulae book.

Example

A number of cocker spaniel puppies are randomly selected at a large kennels. The age, in weeks, and the area of its right ear in cm², of each is obtained. The results are recorded below.

Puppy	A	B	C	D	E	F	G
Age: w weeks	2	4	8	9	10	12	15
Right ear: e cm²	6	18	45	57	68	112	245

[you may quote without giving any justification: $\Sigma w^2 = 634$; $\Sigma e^2 = 82\,827$; $\Sigma we = 6656$]

a) Determine: S_{ww}, S_{ee} and S_{we}.

b) Calculate the product moment correlation coefficient between the puppy's age and the area of its right ear.

c) Comment on your finding in b)

d) How would your answer to b) change if the age were measured in fractions of a year, and the area given in mm²?

Answer

a) $S_{ww} = 634 - \dfrac{(60)^2}{7} \approx 119.7\ldots,$

$S_{ee} = 82\,827 - \dfrac{(551)^2}{7} \approx 39\,455.4\ldots$

$S_{we} = 6656 - \dfrac{60 \times 551}{7} \approx 1933.1$

b) $r \approx 0.889\ldots$

c) There is a strong positive relationship between age and area of right ear. The older a puppy is the larger the area of its right ear.

d) There would be no change.

Exam tips

Ensure you are aware of any deviation from the (x, y) notation.

Exam tips

Use your calculator to find Σw and Σe and to store exact values of S_{ww}, S_{ee}, and S_{we} for subsequent use.

Mention the nature of the relationship and interpret this in context.

Pearson's pmcc is unaffected by a change in units used for either variable, nor does coding affect the value of r.

Stop and think 1

Refer back to Figures 3.2, 3.3 and 3.4. The values of the product moment correlation coefficient have been mislaid. A researcher finds a scrap of paper with three negative numbers on it: −0.4, −0.07, −0.8. It is believed these may be the three pmcc for the sets of data, but which value corresponds to which relationship?

Explanatory and response variables

In none of the above discussion relating to correlation is there any sense that one of the variables gives rise to the other variable. It is **not possible** to infer **causation** from correlation. It would be wrong to conclude that one variable causes changes in the other variable even when the correlation coefficient is close to +1 or −1.

Imagine a situation where children are chosen at random from primary and secondary schools. The data collected from each child are: age in years and months, span of each hand in cm, a mathematical knowledge score and a literacy skills assessment.

Subsequent analysis of the data reveals a strong positive correlation between the spans of the left and right hands. Clearly this does not imply that having a small right hand span causes a person to have a small left hand span. A person's hands are usually very similar in size, hence the strong positive correlation.

A strong positive correlation is found between a child's average hand span and their mathematical knowledge. Older children have larger hands and have greater exposure to mathematics. It is likely that these two variables are correlated through a third variable namely the age of the child, the older the child the more mathematics to which they have been exposed.

The correlation between mathematical knowledge and literacy assessment is also strong and positive. In this case there might be an argument that the more literate a person is – in other words the better their reading skills – the more they are able to gain from reading other subjects. It is reasonable to propose that a child's literacy skills are a **factor** in their mathematical knowledge. In the above example, literacy skills assessment is said to be the **explanatory variable** upon which mathematical knowledge depends. The mathematical knowledge score is said to be the **response variable** dependent upon the child's literacy skills. This does not, however, arise from the correlation but from the interpretation of the factors.

Essential notes

The terms: predictor, factor, explanatory variable, independent variable, are commonly taken to be synonymous. Response variable, dependent variable are synonymous.

Stop and think 2

Analysis of the children's data showed a strong correlation between the literacy skills assessment and age. Assume it is reasonable to consider these two variables as constituting a factor–response pair, which is the explanatory variable?

Least squares regression

This section focuses on determining the most appropriate equation to **model** a linear relationship between two variables. It is vitally important to have decided accurately which of the variables concerned is the response, and which is the explanatory variable. These variables are not interchangeable in the derivation of the equation representing the linear relationship.

Consider a situation where the depth of water flowing under a bridge is measured and plotted against the total of the previous week's rainfall. It is clear that the rainfall does not depend on the depth of water. The only reasonable relationship is that the depth of water under the bridge depends on the week's rainfall.

Exam tips

Never confuse explanatory and response variables.

Essential notes

Rainfall is the independent variable, depth of water is the dependent variable.

Regression of *y* on *x*

In seeking a linear model for the relationship between a response variable (*y*) and an explanatory variable (*x*) the **'least squares'** line of regression of *y* on *x* is a popular choice. This model has the property that the line passes through the 'mean point', in other words, it passes through a point with coordinates $(\bar{x}, \bar{y})$. Its gradient is the ratio $\dfrac{S_{xy}}{S_{xx}}$.

Essential notes

You will be familiar with $y = mx + c$ as the equation of a straight line

These two features are sufficient to uniquely determine its equation in the form $y = a + bx$, where:

$$b = \frac{S_{xy}}{S_{xx}}$$

and $a = \bar{y} - b\bar{x}$

The term 'least squares' refers to the straight line that minimizes the sum of the squares of the vertical distances from the line to each of the data points. These vertical distances are known as **residuals**. The regression line, therefore, makes the sum of the squares of the residuals as small as possible. A data point which has a large residual may have its accuracy called into question. Plotting a scattergraph of the data and superimposing the regression line can be useful in identifying possible anomalies.

Exam tips

Make sure you recall how to plot a straight line graph from its equation.

Fig. 3.6
Age of children and waking hours

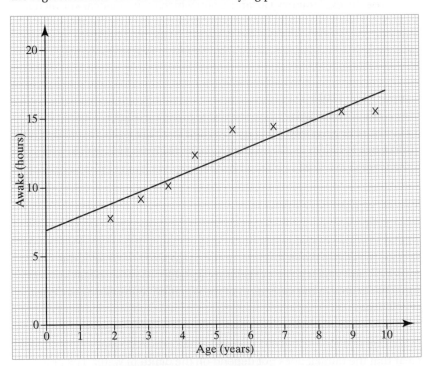

A group of one-child families was asked about the age of their child and the number of hours their child spent awake the previous day. The results are presented in the scattergraph in Figure 3.6.

The child who is aged about 5.5 years has the largest residual. A researcher might want to revisit the data records (or the family) to check the accuracy of the information.

These data have had the line of regression of 'waking hours on age' superimposed. The gradient is approximately 1 (hour per year) and it crosses the y axis at about 7 years.

Example

A young motorcycle enthusiast kept records of the winning speed of the local annual 800 cc road race. These are shown in the table for ten consecutive years:

Year, x	1	2	3	4	5	6	7	8	9	10
Speed, y mph	108.8	109.1	110.3	113.1	117.4	121.4	114.3	121.2	123.9	126.9

[you may assume $\Sigma x = 55$, $\Sigma y = 1166.4$, $\Sigma xy = 6579.5$, $\Sigma x^2 = 385$]

Determine the equation of regression of y on x, giving the coefficients accurate to 3 significant figures.

Answer

You need to calculate the gradient $b = \dfrac{S_{xy}}{S_{xx}}$, before you can find '$a$'

Here:

$$S_{xy} = 6579.5 - \frac{55 \times 1166.4}{10} = 164.3$$

and $S_{xx} = 385 - \dfrac{55^2}{10} = 82.5$, hence $b = \dfrac{164.3}{82.5} = 1.991515\ldots$

Now it is possible to determine 'a' using 'b', and the 'mean point':

$$a = \frac{1166.4}{10} - \frac{55}{10} \times 1.991515\ldots = 105.6866\ldots$$

This leads to the equation: $y = 106 + 1.99x$

Exam tips
Make sure you store both S_{xy} and S_{xx} as accurately as possible in your calculator.

Uses of the regression equation

The regression coefficients, 'a' and 'b', have the same role as the 'intersection' and 'gradient' in the equation of a straight line. Their interpretation must be made in the context of the data. In the above example of the annual road race winning speeds, an appropriate interpretation of the two coefficients might be as follows. The gradient, 1.99, represents the annual increase in the winning speed. Its units would be 1.99 mph per year. The intersection, 106, represents the hypothetical winning speed with $x = 0$, which would be the year before the records started.

Essential notes

In the form $y = mx + c$, m is the gradient and c is the intersection with the y axis.

Interpretation of the gradient is a fair and reasonable process to engage in, but caution is needed when interpreting the value of 'a'. The equation is strictly valid only for values of x within the range of the data. In the case of the road race data, $x = 0$, is not in the data's range. This is particularly evident in the case of the waking hours data – the intersection suggests that a newly born baby will spend 7 hrs awake on day one of its life.

Use of the regression equation to predict values for the response variable is **valid** when **interpolating** (that is, for values of the explanatory variable within the range of the data). It is **not valid** to use the regression equation to **extrapolate** (in other words, to find predicted values of the response variable for values of the explanatory variable outside the data's range). So you would use the regression equation with extreme caution if extrapolating – the results are unlikely to be reliable.

Essential notes

Interpolation is reasonable, **extrapolation** is unreliable.

Example

Return to the road race data.

a) Plot the data on a scatter diagram and draw the line of regression of winning speed on year.

b) It is known that the speed for one of the years was wrongly recorded. Suggest which year this might be, stating the reason for your selection.

c) Evaluate the four summations, Σx, Σy, Σxy, Σx^2, with the data for your chosen year removed, and hence determine a new equation for the regression of winning speed on year.

d) Use the equation derived in part (iii) to predict

    i) the speed in year 7

    ii) the speed in year 20

e) Comment on the two predictions in part (d).

Answer

a)

Fig. 3.7
Scattergraph and regression line

b) The winning speed for year 7 is a long way from the regression line. This suggests that this data point may be in error.

c) $\Sigma x = 55 - 7 = 48$; $\Sigma y = 1166.4 - 114.3 = 1052.1$; $\Sigma xy = 6579.5 - 7 \times 114.3 = 5779.4$, $\Sigma x^2 = 385 - 7^2 = 336$

This leads to the new gradient: $\dfrac{5779.4 - \dfrac{48 \times 1052.1}{9}}{336 - \dfrac{48^2}{9}} = 2.1025$

and a new $'a' = \dfrac{1052.1}{9} - \dfrac{49}{9} \times 2.1025 \approx 105.69\ldots$

Hence, the new equation is: $y = 106 + 2.10x$

d) i) $y(7) = 105.69\ldots + 2.1025 \times 7 = 120.404\ldots = 120$ mph

   ii) $y(20) \approx 148$ mph

e) The predicted winning speed in year 7 is likely to be reasonably close to what it actually was, however the prediction for year 20 is unreliable because 20 is outside the range of the x-values.

Exam tips

Store the full calculator values for 'b' and 'a'.

Exam tips

Use the calculator stored values at this point.

Coding

In the section on the product moment correlation coefficient you saw that its value was unchanged by a change in units. This is equivalent to saying that r does not vary under linear coding of either or both sets of units. Unfortunately, this is not the case for the equation of the line of regression.

Consider, in the above example, what would happen to the equation if the speed were required to be expressed in km per hour (kph). There are 1.6093 km in one mile, so y mph would be z kph where $z = 1.6093 \times y$. This leads to the new equation: $z = (105.69\ldots + 2.1025x) \times 1.6093 = 170.08\ldots + 3.3835x$

in other words $z = 170 + 3.38x$.

Example

Given that $44.704 \text{ ms}^{-1} \equiv 100$ mph, rewrite the equation $y(\text{mph}) = 106 + 2.10x$ to give the speed in metres per second

Answer

$z(\text{ms}^{-1}) = (106 + 2.10x) \times 0.44704 \therefore z = 47.4 + 0.940x$

Essential notes

Where there is no discernible relationship the value of r will be close to zero. But a value of r close to zero does not imply no relationship.

Stop and think 3

Concert violinists retune their violin strings during intermissions between performances. The temperature in a concert hall can change over a performance. This gives rise to a change in tension of the strings. As a result, the pitch of the strings changes. An experiment is carried out using the E string of a violin. It is pre-tensioned ahead of the experiment. Its pitch is subsequently measured at various temperatures.

State, with a reason, which of the variables in the experiment is the explanatory variable.

Method notes

Imagine placing axes at the 'mean point' on each graph. Then 'top right' and 'bottom left' quadrants give positive contributions. The other two quadrants give negative contributions

Stop and think answers

Answer 1

Fig. 3.2: –0.8

Fig. 3.3: –0.4

Fig. 3.4: –0.07

It is worth noting that in Figure 3.4 there appears to be a clear relationship between the variables (perhaps quadratic) yet the correlation coefficient is virtually zero. For Figure 3.2 the correlation coefficient has a large magnitude, yet the relationship between temperature and time is better modelled as a negative exponential rather than a linear one. In Figure 3.3 the majority of the data show little or no relationship, the two data points corresponding to the minimum and maximum heights have a substantial influence on the value of the correlation coefficient.

Method notes

The older a child gets, the greates their skills in reading and writing.

Answer 2

Age is the explanatory variable.

Method notes

It is clearly wrong to think that changes in pitch would alter the temperature of the surroundings.

Answer 3

Temperature, because changes in this give rise to changes in pitch.

Probability function and cumulative distribution function

Discrete random variable

In a statistical experiment where the possible outcomes are distinct, or definitive, or discrete values, the possibilities are called '**discrete data**'. Such values are often positive integers, for example the possible outcomes on a cuboid die: 1, 2, 3, 4, 5, 6. Discrete data might also be counts such as the number of tomatoes a gardener harvests from each plant in the greenhouse: 5, 6, 7, ... 10, ... 15, ... 20. Discrete data do not have to be integers, for example an experiment investigating shoe sizes might result in outcomes such as 6, 7½, 8, 8½, 9½, 10.

A **discrete random variable** is a **model** which provides a distinct value to every possible outcome for a statistical experiment. A capital letter is often used to represent a defined random variable. For example, the outcomes on a cuboid die might be represented by the random variable X. Then $X = \{1, 2, 3, 4, 5, 6\}$. It is more of a challenge to define the random variable representing the shoe size possibilities. Here an assumption needs to be made about the minimum and maximum sizes, say 5 and 11. Then the random variable would be Y where $Y = \{5, 5½, 6, 6½, 7, 7½, 8, 8½, 9, 9½, 10, 10½, 11\}$.

Each statistical experiment has its own frequency distribution, and when this is divided by the total number of observations, a **relative frequency distribution** results. In the case of the random variable, X, defined above, you might anticipate that each outcome would occur with the same relative frequency, $\frac{1}{6}$. This is represented in a mathematical model called a **probability distribution**.

Probability distribution and probability function

There are a number of ways of presenting a probability distribution. A common approach is to use a table showing all the outcomes and their associated probabilities:

Outcome	1	2	3	4	5	6
Probability	$\frac{1}{6}$	$\frac{1}{6}$	$\frac{1}{6}$	$\frac{1}{6}$	$\frac{1}{6}$	$\frac{1}{6}$

An alternative approach employs a **probability function**, $P(X = x)$ where x is any one of the outcomes. In this case, where $x = 1, 2, 3, 4, 5$ or 6, the probability function would look like:

$$P(X = x) = \frac{1}{6}.$$

Example

A red and a green unbiased tetrahedral die have their faces numbered 1, 2, 3, 4. An experiment consists of rolling the two dice and recording the number face down on each die. A random variable, X, is defined as the sum of the outcomes on the two faces.

a) Complete the sample space for X below:

4				8	
3	4		6		
2	3	4			
1	2	3	4		
R / G	1	2	3	4	

Fig. 4.1
Sample space for sum of outcomes

b) The probability distribution for X is shown in the table:

x	2	3	4	5	6	7	8
$P(X=x)$	$\frac{1}{16}$	$\frac{1}{8}$	$\frac{3}{16}$	a	b	c	$\frac{1}{16}$

Find the values of a, b, and c.

c) The probability function can be expressed as

$$P(X = x) = \begin{cases} \dfrac{x - d}{16} & x = 2, 3, 4, 5 \\ \dfrac{e - x}{16} & x = 6, 7, 8 \end{cases}$$

Determine the values of d and e.

Answer

a)

4	5	6	7	8
3	4	5	6	7
2	3	4	5	6
1	2	3	4	5
R / G	1	2	3	4

Fig. 4.2
Completed sample space diagram

b) The sample space shows that, out of 16 combinations, there are 4 ways in which $X=5$, hence the probability is that $a = \dfrac{4}{16}$, similarly there are 3 ways in which $X=6$ and 2 in which $X=7$ therefore $b = \dfrac{3}{16}$ and $c = \dfrac{2}{16}$

Essential notes

Each individual outcome in the sample space is equally likely.

c) Compare the actual probabilities with the function $P(X=x)$. For example we know that $P(X=2) = \dfrac{1}{16}$ so if this $= \dfrac{2-d}{16}$ Check this with, say $x=5$

$$\Rightarrow d = 1$$

Similarly, try $P(X=8) = \dfrac{1}{16} = \dfrac{e-8}{16}$ to determine that $e = 9$

Essential notes

$$\sum_{all\,possibilities} P(X = x_i) = 1$$

In the example of the red and green dice, the outcomes might have been listed as $x_1 = 2, x_2 = 3, \dots, x_7 = 8$

Properties of probability function

A discrete random variable represents all possible outcomes, and the probability function provides the associated probabilities. This gives rise to two properties:

a) probability is a number lying between zero and one, hence, $0 \le P(X=x) \le 1$

b) since the probability associated with certainty is one, the sum of all probabilities comes to 1.

Example

A discrete random variable, X, has values with associated probabilities shown in the table:

x_i	0	1	2	3
$P(X=x_i)$	k	$2k$	$2k$	k

Determine the value of k, hence find $P(X>0)$.

Answer

$\sum_i P(X = x_i)$ must total one, hence $k + 2k + 2k + k = 1$.

This leads to $k = \dfrac{1}{6}$

Therefore $P(X>0) = \dfrac{2}{6} + \dfrac{2}{6} + \dfrac{1}{6} = \dfrac{5}{6}$

Cumulative distribution function

In Chapter 1 you met the concept of cumulative frequency in relation to a frequency distribution. Where random variables are concerned, the equivalent mathematical model is the **cumulative distribution function**. This is represented by a capital letter, typically $F(x)$. The cumulative distribution function is $F(x) = P(X \le x)$.

Example

The cumulative distribution function for a discrete random variable, X, is given by:

$$F(x) = \begin{cases} \dfrac{x}{20} & x = 1, 2, \ldots, 20 \\ 1 & x > 20 \\ 0 & x < 1 \end{cases}$$

Find the following:

a) $P(X < 10)$

b) $P(8 < X \leq 15)$

c) $P(X > 16)$.

Answer

a) X is a discrete random variable. This implies that $P(X < 10) \equiv P(X \leq 9)$ and this implies that the cumulative distribution function can be used: $P(X \leq 9) = F(9) = \dfrac{9}{20}$

b) $P(8 < X \leq 15) \equiv P(X \leq 15) - P(X \leq 8) = F(15) - F(8)$, which implies that the cumulative distribution function can now be used to give $\dfrac{15}{20} - \dfrac{8}{20} = \dfrac{7}{20}$

c) $P(X > 16) \equiv 1 - P(X \leq 16) = 1 - \dfrac{16}{20} = \dfrac{1}{5}$

Exam tips

Take great care in considering strict inequalities and inclusive inequalities for discrete variables.

Exam tips

Recall the concept of complementary events: $X > 16$ and $X \leq 16$ are complementary.

Mean and variance

In Chapter 1 you met the mean for a frequency distribution: $x = \dfrac{\Sigma xf}{n}$ where $n = \Sigma f$.

Here is a reminder.

Example

The results of rolling an unbiased die 40 times are shown in the table:

x	1	2	3	4	5	6
f	5	6	9	8	7	5

Find the mean outcome for the experiment.

Answer

$$\text{Mean} = \frac{\Sigma xf}{n} = \frac{1 \times 5 + 2 \times 6 + \ldots 6 \times 5}{40} = 3.525$$

Now consider approaching the above calculation in a slightly different way. Rather than leaving the division by 40 until the end of the process, divide the frequencies by 40 first. This gives the experimental probabilities for each outcome as shown in the table over the page.

p	$\dfrac{5}{40}$	$\dfrac{6}{40}$	$\dfrac{9}{40}$	$\dfrac{8}{40}$	$\dfrac{7}{40}$	$\dfrac{5}{40}$

Now sum the values $x \times p$, that is, $\sum x \times p$, or more formally, $\sum x \times P(X = x)$ to give:

$$1 \times \frac{5}{40} + 2 \times \frac{6}{40} + \ldots + 6 \times \frac{5}{40} = 3.525.$$

The above summation, $\sum xp$, is the basis of finding the mean for a discrete random variable. A special symbol is used for the mean of a random variable, μ: $\mu = \sum_{allx} xP(X = x)$

Essential notes

The symbol μ is the lower case 'm' from the Greek alphabet. It is pronounced 'mu'.

Example

A random variable, Y, has the following probability distribution:

y	1	2	3
$P(Y = y)$	0.5	0.3	0.2

Calculate the mean of Y.

Answer

$\sum yP(Y = y) = 1 \times 0.5 + 2 \times 0.3 + 3 \times 0.2 = 1.7$

Variance

In Chapter 1 you met variance in connection with standard deviation as a measure of dispersion. This implies that, for a frequency distribution, its variance $Var(X)$, which is the average squared deviation from the mean, is obtained by dividing S_{xx} by n giving: $\dfrac{S_{xx}}{n} = \dfrac{\sum x^2 f}{n} - \dfrac{(\sum xf)^2}{n^2}$ which

$$= \sum x^2 \left(\frac{f}{n}\right) - \left(\sum x\frac{f}{n}\right)^2.$$

This can thus be expressed in probability terms as:

Variance $= \sum x^2 p - (\sum xp)^2$ where $\dfrac{f}{n} = p$.

This is the form that you are most likely to find useful in calculating the variance of a discrete random variable.

A special symbol, σ^2, is used for the variance of a random variable.

Essential notes

Recall $S_{xx} = \sum x^2 f - \dfrac{(\sum xf)^2}{n}$

$Var(X) = \sum x^2 P(X = x) - \mu^2$ is given in your formulae book.

σ 'sigma' is the lower case Greek 's'. Recall that standard deviation is $\sqrt{\text{variance}}$, this implies that σ is the standard deviation of a random variable.

Example

A discrete random variable, X, has its probability function, $P(X = x)$, defined by:

$$P(X = x) = \begin{cases} \dfrac{x^2}{28} & x = 1, 2, 3 \\ \dfrac{(7 - x)^2}{28} & x = 4, 5, 6 \end{cases}$$

a) Determine its mean, μ

b) Hence, calculate its variance, σ^2

c) Find $P(\mu - \sigma < X < \mu + \sigma)$

Answer

a) The mean

$$\mu = \sum_{all\,x} xP(X = x)$$

$$= 1 \times \frac{1}{28} + 2 \times \frac{4}{28} + 3 \times \frac{9}{28} + 4 \times \frac{(7 - 4)^2}{28} + 5 \times \frac{(7 - 5)^2}{28} + 6 \times \frac{(7 - 6)^2}{28}$$

$$= 3.5$$

b) The variance

$$\sigma^2 = \sum_{all\,x} x^2 P(X = x) - \mu^2$$

$$= 1^2 \times \frac{1}{28} + 2^2 \times \frac{4}{28} + 3^2 \times \frac{9}{28} + 4^2 \times \frac{9}{28} + 5^2 \times \frac{4}{28} + 6^2 \times \frac{1}{28} - (3.5)^2$$

$$= 1.25$$

c) From the above answers, $\mu - \sigma = 3.5 - \sqrt{1.25} \approx 2.38$ and $\mu + \sigma = 4.62$, and so $P(\mu - \sigma < X < \mu + \sigma)$ becomes $P(3 \leq X \leq 4)$ since it is a discrete variable

$$P(\mu - \sigma < X < \mu + \sigma) \equiv P(X = 3) + P(X = 4) - \frac{18}{28}$$

Exam tips

You might have examined the probabilities and seen that X is symmetrically distributed, so $\mu = 3.5$ from symmetry.

Exam tips

This is a discrete random variable, so there is no case for rounding.

Functions of a random variable

Statisticians often use a concept known as **expectation** in dealing with random variables. For example, earlier you met the mean, μ, of a discrete random variable, X. This is also called the **expected value** of X. This is represented by the notation $E(X)$. So, μ and $E(X)$ are the same and they represent the mean of a random variable. You need to be aware that the expected value is the same as the mean.

At a May Fayre stall a contestant pays 20p and is allowed to shuffle a pack of 52 playing cards. If the top card is the ace of hearts the contestant receives a pound coin as their prize. They get a 50p coin if the top card is any other ace. If the card is not an ace they receive no prize.

How much might the stallholder **expect to gain** from running this stall?

The answer depends on how many people play the game and what cards appear on top of the pack at each shuffle. Finding the average gain (**mean gain**) per 'go' will be sufficient because if this is positive, then in the long run, the stallholder will benefit.

Set up a discrete random variable, X, representing the gain to the stallholder. This can take any one of three different values with the probabilities shown in the table over the page.

x pence	20	−30	−80
P(X = x)	$\dfrac{48}{52}$	$\dfrac{3}{52}$	$\dfrac{1}{52}$

Then the expected gain is:

$$E(X) = \mu = \Sigma x P(X = x)$$

$$= 20 \times \frac{48}{52} + -30 \times \frac{3}{52} + -80 \times \frac{1}{52}$$

$$= \frac{790}{52} \approx 15.2$$

The stallholder can expect to gain just over 15p for each 'go' at the game. In the above situation, the expected gain and the mean gain are readily seen to be equivalent concepts.

Coding

Return to the May Fayre scenario. A second stall sets up a similar game but with a 50p stake and prizes of £5.00 and £2.50. What is the relationship between the random variable, Y, representing the gain to the second stall and the random variable, X? What is the expected gain to the second stall?

Corresponding values of X and Y are shown in the table:

x pence	+20	−30	−80
y pence	+50	−200	−450

The relationship between Y and X needs to be established: check that you agree that it is $Y = 5X − 50$. A direct consequence of this is the relationship between their expected values: $E(Y) = 5E(X) − 50$. Thus the second stallholder expects to gain almost 26p per 'go'.

This scenario serves to illustrate that the **coding**, $Y = aX + b$, leads to $E(Y) = aE(X) + b$.

What happens to the variance under coding? This is illustrated by returning to the May Fayre scenario.

The variance of the first stall is:

$$\text{var}(X) = \sum_{all\,x} x^2 P(X = x) - (E(X))^2$$

$$= 20^2 \times \frac{48}{52} + (-30)^2 \times \frac{3}{52} + (-80)^2 \times \frac{1}{52} - \left(\frac{790}{52}\right)^2$$

$$\approx 313.42\ldots$$

and the variance of the second stall is:

$$\text{var}(Y) = \sum_{all\,y} y^2 P(Y = y) - (E(Y))^2$$

$$= 50^2 \times \frac{48}{52} + (-200)^2 \times \frac{3}{52} + (-450)^2 \times \frac{1}{52} - \left(\frac{1350}{52}\right)^2$$

$$\approx 7835.61\ldots$$

Thus the variance of Y is exactly 25 times the variance of X. The relationship between the two random variables is $Y = 5X − 50$. Only the scale factor, 5, plays a part in influencing the variance.

Essential notes

It is worth checking that:

$\Sigma y P(Y = y)$ which is $5 \times 15.2 - 50$

$= 50 \times \dfrac{48}{52} - 200 \times \dfrac{3}{52} - 450 \times \dfrac{1}{52}$

$= 25.96\ldots \approx 26.0$

Exam tips

Make sure you square the values of x and not the probabilities.

Exam tips

You need to know the two results for coding $Y = aX + b$:

$E(Y) = aE(X) + b$

$\text{Var}(Y) = a^2\,\text{Var}(X)$.

In fact, it is the square of the scale factor that is needed.

$\text{var}(Y) = 5^2 \times \text{var}(X).$

Example

The probability distribution for a random variable, X, is shown in the table:

x	1	2	3	4
$P(X = x)$	0.5	0.3	0.15	0.05

Determine

a) $E(X)$,

b) $\text{var}(X)$,

c) $E(5 - 2X)$,

d) $\text{var}(5 - 2X)$.

Answer

a) $E(X) = 1.75$

b) $\text{var}(X) = 1^2 \times 0.5 + 2^2 \times 0.3 + 3^2 \times 0.15 + 4^2 \times 0.05 - (1.75)^2 = 0.7875$

c) $E(5 - 2X) = 5 - 2 \times 1.75 = 1.5$

d) $\text{var}(5 - 2X) = (-2)^2 \times \text{var}(X) = 3.15$

Exam tips

Square the values of x not probability.

Use the coding results you have learned.

Independent observation

Where independent observations are made of random variables we rely on the concept of statistical independence introduced in Chapter 2. The random variables concerned may be the same or different.

For example, two people play a game where each rolls an ordinary unbiased die with faces numbered 1 to 6. Let X_1, be the random variable representing the outcome on the first die and X_2, be the outcome on the second die. A joint event can be defined where the first die shows a specified number and the second die shows another number (which can be the same). For example, $X_1 = 5$ and $X_2 = 6$ is a joint event. This is a joint event where the sum of the outcomes is 11. To determine the probability of **joint events**, you can use **statistical independence**.

$P(X_1 = 5 \text{ and } X_2 = 6) = P(X_1 = 5) \times P(X_2 = 6) = \dfrac{1}{6} \times \dfrac{1}{6} = \dfrac{1}{36}$

Essential notes

Recall that for independent events A, B:
$P(A \cap B) = P(A) \times P(B).$

In addition, the concept of **mutual exclusion** might be called upon. To determine the probability that the total of the two dice comes to 11, you need to consider all the possible ways that this could occur:

$P(X_1 + X_2 = 11) = P((X_1 = 5 \text{ and } X_2 = 6) \text{ or } (X_1 = 6 \text{ and } X_2 = 5))$
$= P(X_1 = 5 \text{ and } X_2 = 6) + P(X_1 = 6 \text{ and } X_2 = 5)$
$= \dfrac{1}{36} + \dfrac{1}{36} = \dfrac{1}{18}$

Essential notes

For mutually exclusive events A, B:
$P(A \text{ or } B) = P(A) + P(B).$

Example
The probability distribution for random variable, X, is given in the table:

x	1	2	3
$P(X = x)$	0.2	0.3	0.5

Two independent observations, X_1 and X_2, are made of X. Calculate:

a) $P(X_1 = 2 \text{ and } X_2 = 2)$

b) $P(X_1 + X_2 = 4)$

Answer

a) $P(X_1 = 2 \text{ and } X_2 = 2) = P(X_1 = 2) \times P(X_2 = 2) = 0.3 \times 0.3 = 0.09$

b) There are three mutually exclusive ways in which $P(X_1 + X_2 = 4)$, namely: $X_1 = 2$ and $X_2 = 2$, $X_1 = 1$ and $X_2 = 3$ and $X_1 = 3$ and $X_2 = 1$.

Hence, $P(X_1 + X_2 = 4) = 0.3 \times 0.3 + 0.2 \times 0.5 + 0.5 \times 0.2 = 0.29$

Discrete uniform distribution

A commonly occurring random variable is one where the probability of each outcome is the same. A typical example is the outcome on a fair cuboid die. Here each outcome has the probability $\frac{1}{6}$. Each outcome is equally likely. Where the outcomes of random variable are equally likely, the probabilities are constant and the term 'uniform distribution' is used. A probability graph for a typical uniform distribution is shown in Figure 4.3.

Fig. 4.3
A uniform distribution where
$P(X = x) = 0.125$

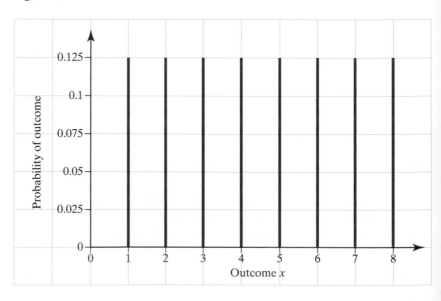

Example

A random variable, X, has cumulative distribution function given by:

$$F(x) = \frac{x}{n} \qquad x = 1, 2, 3, \ldots, n$$

Where n is a positive integer.

Prove that X is a uniformly distributed random variable.

Answer

$F(1) = P(X \leq 1) = P(1) = \frac{1}{n}$.

Let k be an integer such that $1 < k \leq n$. Then:

$$P(X = k) = F(k) - F(k - 1) = \frac{k}{n} - \frac{(k - 1)}{n} = \frac{1}{n}.$$

Thus $P(X = k)$ is a constant and the sum of the probabilities amounts to unity, therefore X is uniformly distributed.

Mean and Variance

A uniform probability distribution has probability function:

$$P(X = x) = \frac{1}{n} \qquad x = 1, 2, \ldots, n$$

The mean, μ, and variance, σ^2, of the random uniform variable, X, are given by:

$$\mu = \frac{n + 1}{2}$$

and

$$\sigma^2 = \frac{n^2 - 1}{12}$$

Example

The outcome on a fair tetrahedral die is modelled by the uniform random variable with probability function

$$P(X = x) = \frac{1}{4} \qquad x = 1, 2, 3, 4$$

A second fair tetrahedral die has the following on its face, 8, 13, 18, 23.

a) Write down:

  i) $E(X)$

  ii) $Var(X)$

b) If Y represents the random variable modelling the outcome on the second die, demonstrate that $Y = aX + b$ where a and b are to be found.

c) Hence, write down:

  i) $E(Y)$

  ii) $Var(Y)$

Essential notes

Recall that the cumulative distribution function is: $P(X \leq x)$.

Exam tips

These formulae are **not** given in the formulae book.

Answer

a) i) $E(X) = \text{mean} = \dfrac{4 + 1}{2} = 2\frac{1}{2}$

ii) $Var(X) = \text{variance} = \dfrac{4^2 - 1}{12} = 1\frac{1}{4}$

b) Assume $Y = aX + b$ then $8 = a \times 1 + b$ and $13 = a \times 2 + b$. Solving these as simultaneous equations gives $a = 5$ and $b = 3$. (Check with 18 and 23.)

c) i) $E(Y) = E(5X + 3) = 5 \times 2\frac{1}{2} + 3 = 15\frac{1}{2}$

ii) $Var(Y) = Var(5X + 3) = 5^2\, Var(X) = 31\frac{1}{4}$

Exam tips

$E(X) = \dfrac{n + 1}{2}$, $\text{var}(X) = \dfrac{n^2 - 1}{12}$

Essential notes

Recall $E(aX + b)$
$= a \times E(X) + b$

$V(aX + b) = a^2 V(X)$.

Fig. 4.4
Sample space for random variable M

Stop and think

The outcome on a blue fair tetrahedral die with faces numbered: 0, 1, 2, 3, is modelled by the random variable B. The random variable, Y, models the outcome on a yellow fair tetrahedral dice with its faces numbered: 1, 2, 3, 4.

The random variable, M, is defined as B × Y.

a) Complete the sample space diagram for M.

Y / B	0	1	2	3
4			8	
3	0		6	
2	0		4	
1	0	1	2	3
	0	1	2	3

b) The outcome space for M is {0, 1, 2, 3, 4, 6, 8, 9, 12}. Write down the associated probability distribution.

c) Calculate:

i) E(M)

ii) Var(M)

Stop and think answer

a)

4	0	4	8	12
3	0	3	6	9
2	0	2	4	6
1	0	1	2	3
Y ╱ B	0	1	2	3

Fig. 4.5
Completed sample space for M

b)

M	0	1	2	3	4	6	8	9	12
P	$\frac{1}{4}$	$\frac{1}{16}$	$\frac{1}{8}$	$\frac{1}{8}$	$\frac{1}{8}$	$\frac{1}{8}$	$\frac{1}{16}$	$\frac{1}{16}$	$\frac{1}{16}$

c) i) $3\frac{3}{4}$

   ii) $12\frac{3}{16}$

Method notes

$E(M) = 0 \times \dfrac{1}{4} + 1 \times \dfrac{1}{16}$

$+ 2 \times \dfrac{1}{8} + \ldots$

$V(M) = 0^2 \times \dfrac{1}{4} + 1^2 \times \dfrac{1}{16}$

$+ \ldots + 12^2 \times \dfrac{1}{16} - (3.75)^2$

Standard normal: shape, probability

Continuous random variable

In Chapter 4 you met the discrete random variable as a general model for discrete data. In this chapter you will meet a **continuous random variable** which serves as a model for continuous data. Continuous data such as the weight of cocker spaniels at birth, the height of girls in Year 9, the hand span of 17 year old males, and so on, are symmetrically distributed with a concentration of measurements close to the mean, and fewer measurements further away from the mean.. If we want to know how likely a measurement is to fall within any particular part of the distribution we can use a random variable known as the **normal probability distribution**.

Recall the small collection of hand spans illustrated in the histogram (Figure 1.3) in Chapter 1. That histogram is repeated in Figure 5.1 with an appropriate normal probability distribution model superimposed. This mathematical model can be seen as an attempt to predict the shape of a histogram based on an exceedingly large collection of hand spans. The histogram becomes smooth, in place of the typically stepped histogram.

Fig. 5.1
A histogram and normal model

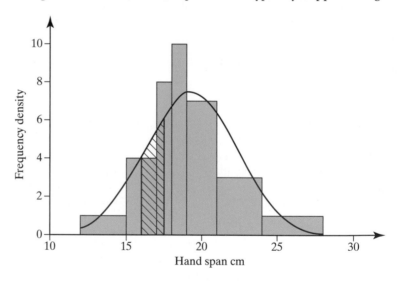

Recall that the vertical axis in a histogram shows frequency density and not frequency. The vertical axis for a continuous random variable measures **probability density** rather than probability. Recall, also, that frequency for continuous data is proportional to the area in a histogram and hence probability, associated with frequency, is found from the area under a probability density function for a continuous random variable. The shaded region in Figure 5.1 under the normal distribution represents the number of hand spans predicted by the model in the interval $16 \leq x < 17.5$.

Standard normal probability density function

The **probability density function** for any normally distributed random variable can be obtained from a distribution known as the **standard**

Essential notes

For a continuous random variable, probability is found from the area under a portion of the density function.

normal. This process will be covered in the section on standardization, below.

The **standard normal random variable** is sufficiently important to have been given its own symbol. A Z-statistic, unless otherwise defined, is one that can be modelled using the **standard normal probability density function**.

Properties of the Z-statistic

Its mean is zero and its standard deviation is one. It is symmetrically distributed, hence its median is also equal to zero, as is its mode. The graph is symmetrical and the mean is the middle value on the horizontal axis.

Essential notes

For any continuous random variable, X, the probability of a specific value occurring is zero.

$P(X = x) = 0$ This is equally true for the: Z-statistic: $P(Z = z) = 0$

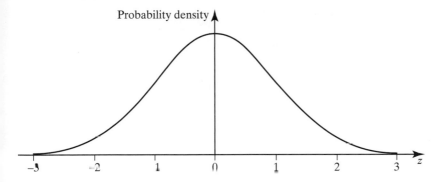

Fig. 5.2
Probability density function for the Z-statistic

Its shape has often been referred to as 'bell shaped' and asymptotic (in other words, the curve approaches the z-axis getting ever closer but never quite reaching it). The area between a section of the curve and the z-axis gives the probability for the relevant section of the z-axis for example the area between the curve, the z-axis and the values $z = 1$ and $z = 2$ would be equivalent to the probability: $P(1 < z < 2)$ or to $P(1 \leq z \leq 2)$ (see Figure 5.4).

The probability that z takes a value of more than 2, that is $P(z > 2)$ cannot be distinguished from the probability that z is at least 2, that is $(z \geq 2)$. The fact that one includes the value 2, and the other does not, makes no difference to the probability. Equally, it means that $P(1 < z < 2)$ is identical to $P(1 \leq z \leq 2)$.

Essential notes

Since z is continuous $P(1 < z < 2) \equiv P(1 \leq z \leq 2)$.

Tables of probabilities

Fortunately much of the work in determining probabilities associated with the Z-statistic has been done for you. Cumulative probabilities, along the lines of the cumulative distribution function (CDF) you met in the first section of Chapter 4 for a discrete random variable, are set out in a table on pages 92–3. The tables show the **cumulative distribution function (CDF)**: $\Phi(z) \equiv P(Z \leq z)$($\Phi$, 'phi' is the Greek capital letter F). This is illustrated in Figure 5.3.

Exam tips

Your calculator might also have the 'standard normal' built into it.

Fig. 5.3
Normal CDF showing
$P(Z < 2) = 0.9772$

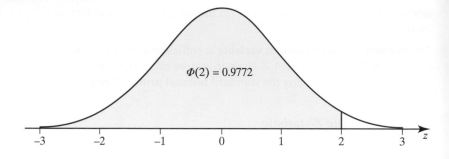

$\Phi(2) = 0.9772$

This means that in order to find $P(1 \leq Z \leq 2)$ you need to look up $P(Z \leq 2)$ and $P(Z \leq 1)$ in the tables and subtract the associated values.

z	Φ(z)
2	0.9772

and

z	Φ(z)
1	0.8413

Fig. 5.4
$P(1 < Z < 2)$ or $P(1 \leq Z \leq 2)$

 $\equiv$ $-$

Exam tips
Round your final answer to
3 s.f.

$$P(1 \leq Z \leq 2) \equiv P(Z \leq 2) - P(Z \leq 1)$$
$$= \Phi(2) - \Phi(1)$$
$$= 0.9772 - 0.8413$$
$$= 0.1359 \approx 0.136$$

Exam tips
It is good practice to start
your answer with a diagram.

Example
Determine the probability that a standard normal variable lies between 0.55 and 2.42.

Answer
The probability required is shown in Figure 5.5. (Sketch the graph by putting in the axes and then drawing the bell curve freehand.)

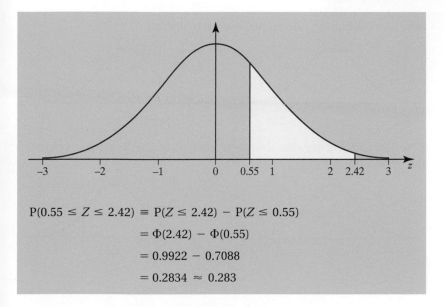

Fig. 5.5
P(0.55 < Z < 2.42)

$$P(0.55 \leq Z \leq 2.42) \equiv P(Z \leq 2.42) - P(Z \leq 0.55)$$
$$= \Phi(2.42) - \Phi(0.55)$$
$$= 0.9922 - 0.7088$$
$$= 0.2834 \approx 0.283$$

Symmetry of the standard normal variable

The statistical tables for the Z-statistic show only values of the cumulative probability when $Z \geq 0$. However it is clear that Z can take values that are less than zero, in other words, negative values.

The symmetry of the probability density function needs to be used when you are finding probabilities associated with $Z < 0$. This is where a simple sketch of the density function and the area (probability) to be determined can be of immense value.

Example
Determine $P(-1.2 < Z < 2.05)$.

Answer
Start with a sketch:

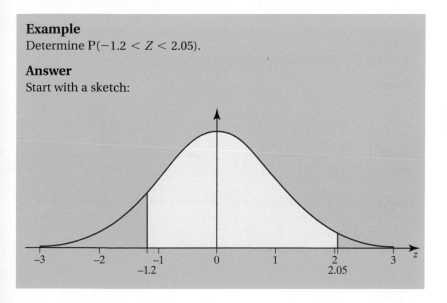

Fig. 5.6
P(−1.2 < Z < 2.05)

Now break this down into cumulative probabilities:

Fig. 5.7
$P(Z < 2.05) - P(Z < -1.2)$

Fig. 5.8
Dealing with a negative Z-value

Now deal with the negative Z-value by making use of the symmetry of the density function:

In dealing with the negative Z-value the final stage makes use of 'complementary events' which were covered in Chapter 2. Finally, put all the parts together to give:

$$P(-1.2 < Z < 2.05) = P(Z < 2.05) - (1 - P(Z < 1.2))$$

$$= 0.9798 - (1 - 0.8849)$$

$$= 0.8647 \approx 0.865$$

[NB: the Z value for 2.05 is halfway between the values for 2.04 and 2.06 given in the tables.]

Example
Calculate the probability: $P(-1.75 < Z < -0.6)$.

Answer

Fig. 5.9
$P(-1.75 < Z < -0.6)$

The symmetry of the density function reveals that this problem is a lot easier than it might seem to be at first sight. The diagrams reveal that it is as simple as: $P(0.6 < Z < 1.75)$. Thus the answer is:
$\Phi(1.75) - \Phi(0.6) = 0.9599 - 0.7257$

$$= 0.2342 \approx 0.234$$

Standardisation

Very few examples of continuous data can be found which are directly modelled by the Z-statistic. However, there are numerous examples of data that can be modelled by the sort of bell-shaped density function seen above, but with a different mean and standard deviation.

Standardising $X \sim N(\mu, \sigma^2)$

Consider a random variable, X, with mean equal to μ and with variance equal to σ^2 (hence standard deviation equal to σ).

This sentence is captured in the mathematical shorthand: $X \sim N(\mu, \sigma^2)$. Values of X can be standardised by subtracting the mean (μ) and dividing the result by the standard deviation (σ):

$$z = \frac{x - \mu}{\sigma}$$

The outcome is a random variable which has its mean equal to zero and its standard deviation equal to one. It is a Z-statistic and therefore the standard normal cumulative distribution tables can be used.

Essential notes

The notation $X \sim N(6, 4)$ would imply $\mu = 6$, $\sigma^2 = 4$

Exam tips

Standardisation involves division by the **standard deviation** not the variance.

Example

Fish from a fish farm are assumed to have a weight which is normally distributed with a mean of 5 kg and a standard deviation 1.5 kg. What is the probability that a randomly caught fish has a weight of more than 8 kg?

Answer

The problem posed is $P(X > 8)$ which is equivalent to the standardised problem $P\left(Z > \dfrac{8 - 5}{1.5}\right)$ for the standard normal variable.

So

$$P(X > 8) \equiv P\left(Z > \frac{8 - 5}{1.5}\right) = P(Z > 2)$$

$$= 1 - P(Z \le 2)$$

$$= 1 - \Phi(2)$$

$$= 1 - 0.9772 = 0.0228$$

This implies that the probability of a fish weighing more than 8 kg is approximately 0.023

Essential notes

This information could also be given as $X \sim N(5, 1.5^2)$ or $X \sim N(5, 2.25)$.

Fig. 5.10
Standardising X

Expected frequencies

In the first section in this chapter (Standard normal: shape, probability) we looked at the hand span data from Chapter 1 and suggested that a normally distributed random variable would be an appropriate model for the distribution of hand spans. Assume that the mean hand span is 19 cm and the standard deviation is 3.0 cm. Use the probability model: $X \sim N(19, 3^2)$ to determine:

a) $P(16 \leq X < 17.5)$

b) the expected number of hand spans in the range
$P(16 \leq \text{hand span} < 17.5)$.

Solution

a) $P(16 \leq X < 17.5) = P(X < 17.5) - P(X < 16)$

$$= P\left(z < \frac{17.5 - 19}{3}\right) - P\left(z \leq \frac{16 - 19}{3}\right)$$

$$= \Phi(-0.5) - \Phi(-1).$$

Fig. 5.11

$\Phi(-\frac{1}{2}) - \Phi(-1)$

 − ≡ −

$$\Phi(-0.5) - \Phi(-1) = \Phi(+1) - \Phi(+0.5)$$

$$= 0.8413 - 0.6915$$

$$\therefore P(16 \leq X < 17.5) = 0.1498 \approx 0.150$$

b) The implications of this probability are that, on average, close to 15% of the hand spans will be in the range 16 cm to 17.5 cm.

Since there was a total of 56 hand spans, the expected number is 15% of 56 which is **8.4.**

Essential notes

Recall there was a total of 56 hand spans.

Exam tips

Expected frequency is an 'average' frequency, it is unlikely to be a whole number.

Comparisons

Standardisation is an effective and reliable method of making **comparisons**. Consider a situation in which a language student, Xaro, has a mark of 58 in Russian studies and a mark of 47 in Ancient Greek. Which is the better performance? Before making the obvious response, it is important to identify the mean and standard deviation of the two mark distributions. These are shown in the table:

	Mean	s.d
Russian	64	3
Ancient Greek	50	2

Assuming that the marks can be modelled by normal distributions, the standardised values of these marks are an indication of their relative merit.

Xaro's standardised mark in Russian studies is: $r = \dfrac{58 - 64}{3} = -2$ and in

Ancient Greek: $g = \dfrac{47 - 50}{2} = -1.5$. This indicates that Xaro's

performance in Russian Studies is relatively poorer than in Ancient Greek. The diagram illustrates this point:

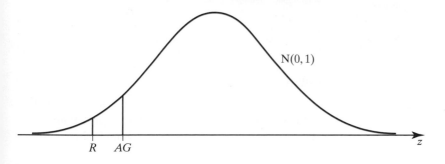

$N(0,1)$

R AG

          z

Fig. 5.12
Standardised marks in Russian
and Greek

Stop and think 1

Refer back to the Russian and Ancient Greek example above. Find the probabilities:

a) P(R < 58)

b) P(G > 47)

Reversing the process

The language student, Xaro, has a standardised mark of +1.25 in French. The marks in French had a mean equal to 63 and a standard deviation equal to 8. What was Xaro's actual mark in French?

Remember that the process of standardising is summarized in the

equation: $z = \dfrac{x - \mu}{\sigma}$ when $X \sim N(\mu, \sigma^2)$. In this case, the various values

involved are: $z = +1.25$, $\mu = 63$, and $\sigma = 8$. This leads to the equation:

$1.25 = \dfrac{x - 63}{8}$

Essential notes

$$1.25 = \frac{x - 63}{8}$$
$$\Rightarrow 8 \times 1.25 = x - 63.$$
$$\Rightarrow \qquad x = 63 + 8 \times 1.25$$

Solving this, by multiplying by 8 then adding 63, gives Xaro's mark in French as 73.

Inverse normal cumulative probability function

Cumulative distribution function

In the first section in this chapter (Standard normal: shape, probability), you saw that the importance of the standard normal random variable was celebrated by calling it a Z-statistic. In addition to this, its probability

Exam tips

You do not need to know the form of the density function.

density function is given as a special symbol: $\phi(z)$; hence, as you have already seen, the associated cumulative distribution function $P(Z < z)$ is represented by the capital letter: $\Phi(z)$.

Example

Determine   a) $\Phi(1.5)$ b) $P(Z > 1.5)$

Answer

a) $\Phi(1.5)$ is exactly the same as the probability: $P(Z < 1.5)$

Hence $\Phi(1.5) = 0.9332$.

b) $P(Z > 1.5) = 1 - \Phi(1.5) = 1 - 0.9332 = 0.0668$

Inverting the cumulative distribution function

Sometimes the CDF needs to be inverted. This section will show when this is necessary and how to do it. $\Phi(z)$ is, from its definition, a probability. Hence, the inverse, $\Phi^{-1}(p)$, is a $Z -$ value. This relationship is shown as:

$p = \Phi(z) \Rightarrow \Phi^{-1}(p) = z$.

For example if $0.9332 = \Phi(z) \Rightarrow \Phi^{-1}(0.9332) = z = 1.5$

Fig. 5.13
Inverse Normal

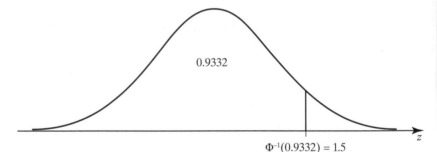

0.9332

$\Phi^{-1}(0.9332) = 1.5$

Another use of tables of the normal distribution function

Your formulae book and statistical tables do not contain separate inverse normal tables. You need to use the standard CDF tables 'backwards', that is you need to invert the tabulated probabilities. For example, to determine $\Phi^{-1}(0.75)$ you need to find the value of Z that gives a cumulative probability of 0.75.

z	$\Phi(z)$
?	0.75

Unfortunately the tables do not show this exactly. What you find is the following:

z	$\Phi(z)$
0.67	0.7486
0.68	0.7517

Exam tips

You are not required to use linear interpolation within these tables.

0.7486 is closer to 0.75 than 0.7517 (0.0014 compared with 0.0017), so the closer answer is taken to be the value of Z corresponding to 0.7486, that is $Z = 0.67$ to (2 d.p.).

Example
Find r, such that $P(Z < r) = 0.8605$

Answer
The relevant part of the normal distribution tables is:

z	Φ(z)
1.08	0.8599
1.09	0.8621

Hence $r = 1.08$, because 0.8605 is closer to 0.8599 than it is to 0.8621

Essential notes
$P(Z < 1.08) = 0.8599$

Inverting the CDF when $X \sim N(\mu, \sigma^2)$
The mean and variance for most problems involving the normal distribution tend to be anything other than zero and one, respectively. For example, suppose the task was to determine the upper quartile height of female undergraduates in England, given that the distribution of their heights, X, is normal with mean equal to 163 cm and standard deviation equal to 6.25 cm, that is $X \sim N(163, 6.25^2)$.

The approach is to standardize the (unknown) upper quartile, invert the Z-tables, then recover the actual height. Let Q stand for quartile:

$$\Phi\left(\frac{Q_3 - 163}{6.25}\right) = 0.75 \Rightarrow \frac{Q_3 - 163}{6.25} \approx 0.67$$

Solving this equation for Q_3 gives $Q_3 \approx 167$ cm

Exam tips
The cumulative probability for the upper quartile is 75% (or 0.75).

Example
Assume that $X \sim N(52, 25)$, find a such that $P(X < a) = 0.925$

Answer
The tables show that $P(Z < 1.44) = 0.9251$, therefore

$$\frac{a - 52}{5} = 1.44 \Rightarrow a = 59.2$$

Exam tips
The notation $N(52, 25)$ indicates $\mu = 52$ and $\sigma^2 = 25$

Example
Assume that $Y \sim N(170, 49)$. Determine:

a) b, where $P(Y > b) = 0.066$

b) c, where $P(Y < c) = 0.055$

Exam tips
Here you have been given 'tail' probabilities. Draw some sketches before you embark on this one.

Fig. 5.14
$P(Y > b)$

Answer

a)

$$P(Y > b) = 0.066 \Rightarrow P(Y \leq b) = 1 - 0.066 = 0.934$$

In the tables you find:

z	Φ(z)
1.50	0.9332
1.51	0.9345

> **Exam tips**
>
> The tables show cumulative probabilities greater than 0.5.

You need a probability of 0.934, the closer value for z is 1.51, so the corresponding Y value is: $\dfrac{b - 170}{7} = 1.51 \Rightarrow b = 180.57$

> **Exam tips**
>
> $N(170, 49)$
> $\Rightarrow \sigma = \sqrt{49}$

Fig 5.15
$P(Y < c)$ and $P(Y > c)$

b)

Bear in mind that, since the region concerned is to the left of the mean, the corresponding Z-value will be negative (that is, to the left of the Z-mean which is zero). However, the tables show only positive Z-values, so the complement to 0.055 (0.945) is needed. The relevant section is:

z	Φ(z)
1.59	0.9441
1.60	0.9452

> **Exam tips**
>
> Notice that this is the correct side of the mean.

This shows that $P(Z < 1.60) = 0.9452$ which implies that $P(Z < -1.60) = 0.0548$. This is as close to 0.055 as the tables allow.

The final step leads to: $\dfrac{c - 170}{7} = -1.60 \Rightarrow c = 158.8$

Improving accuracy

As pointed out above, tables of the normal distribution function, $\Phi(z)$, have been developed in order to determine probabilities, rather than the inverse process. As a result, there are many occasions where you do not find the exact probability you seek, for example in the last example the Z-value for 0.945 was needed but the best the tables revealed was 0.9452, so the Z-value corresponding to this was used.

Tables designed around cumulative probabilities are needed in order to improve accuracy in such circumstances. These are available, but in a somewhat limited fashion. In addition, the tables you have available in the formulae book link the **upper tail probabilities** called '**percentage points of the normal distribution**' with the relevant Z-value for a limited set of probabilities.

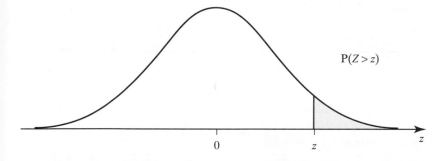

$P(Z > z)$

Fig. 5.16
Upper tail probability

Example

A random variable, X, is normally distributed with $\mu = 73$ and $\sigma = 9$. Determine d if 5% of the random variable is known to exceed d.

Answer

The phrase '5% exceeds d' implies that $P(X > d) = 0.05$. This is one of the upper tail probabilities where you have a more accurate Z-value. The tables indicate directly that $P(Z > 1.6449) = 0.05$. This implies that

the standardised value of d satisfies the equation $\dfrac{d - 73}{9} = 1.6449$.

Solving this gives: $d = 87.8041 \approx 87.8$

Exam tips

Familiarise yourself with the set of upper tail probabilities in the tables.

Whilst the set of percentage points is rather limited, it is worth realizing that complementary probabilities can be tackled and so can lower tail probabilities.

Example

Flint chippings are sold in bags. The weight, W kg, in a bag can be modelled as: $W \sim N(40, 2.25)$.

a) It is know that 99% of bags weigh less that a kg. Determine a.

b) Find b if $P(W > b) = 0.80$

Answer

a) Start by sketching the information supplied:

Fig. 5.17
99% less than a

Remember that the 'percentage points' tables show the upper tail probability, so you need the complement of 0.99 which is 0.01. The tables reveal that: $P(Z > 2.3263) = 0.01$. This implies that the standardized value of a satisfies:

$$\frac{a - 40}{\sqrt{2.25}} = 2.3263 \Rightarrow a = 43.489 \text{ hence } a \approx 43.5$$

b) Again a sketch helps

Fig. 5.18
$P(W > b) = 0.80$

This clearly indicates that b is less than the mean. The lower tail in this case would have a probability of 0.20 which is one of the 'percentage points' tabulated values.

p	z
0.2	0.8416

This tells you that the Z-value corresponding to the upper tail is 0.8416, which means that the value corresponding to the lower tail is -0.8416.

Exam tips

$N(40, 2.25)$
$\Rightarrow \sigma = 1.5.$

Exam tips

The Z-value needed here has to be less than zero.

Hence the standardized value of b satisfies the equation:

$$\frac{b - 40}{1.5} = -0.8416$$

$$\Rightarrow \quad b = 38.7376$$

Hence, $b \approx 38.7$

Determining mean or variance

There are instances where a random variable is known to be normally distributed but the value of the mean or the standard deviation (or both) is not known. When you have information about the probabilities, it is possible to determine the unknown parameter(s).

Example
A jam jar manufacturer models the weight (g) of finished jars by a normal random variable, $G \sim N(\mu, 16)$. The manufacturer observes that 2% of the finished jars weigh more than 250.2 g. Determine the mean, μ.

Answer
Summarize the information in a sketch:

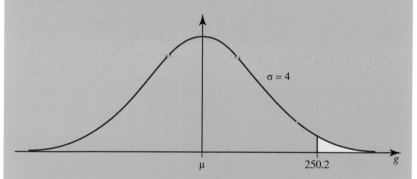

The table of percentage points for the standard normal variable shows that $P(Z > 2.0537) = 0.02$.

p	z
0.02	2.0537

The standardized value of 250.2 satisfies the equation:

$$\frac{250.2 - \mu}{4} = 2.0537$$

Multiply by 4 to give: $250.2 - \mu = 8.2148$

Solving this for μ gives: $\mu = 241.9852 \approx 242.0$ g.

Essential notes

$N(\mu, 16)$ implies that the standard deviation is $\sqrt{16}$

Fig. 5.19
$P(G > 250.2) = 0.02$

Fig. 5.20
70% exceeds 240.3

Example

A new process is introduced in the jam jar factory. This changes the variance so that the weight of the jars is now modelled by the random variable $J \sim N(242, \sigma^2)$. Observation of the new jars reveals that 70% of them have a weight above 240.3 g. Determine the variance of the random variable.

Answer

A sketch:

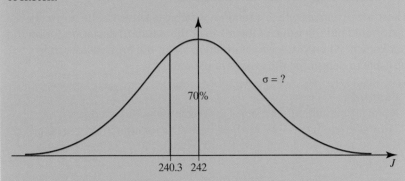

The percentage points tables can be used since the tail probability for this is 30% or 0.3.

p	z
0.3	0.5244

The corresponding value for Z is 0.5244 but this is for an upper tail. Figure 5.20 clearly indicates that there is 30% in the lower tail, so the Z-value required is negative (-0.5244).

Putting all this together gives the following equation for the standard deviation:

$$\frac{240.3 - 242}{\sigma} = -0.5244$$

Multiplying by σ gives: $-1.7 = -0.5244\sigma$

Dividing by: -0.5244 shows that $\sigma = 3.2418\ldots$

Hence, the variance, σ^2, is 10.5

Essential notes

Review how to solve simultaneous equations.

The two examples above illustrate the case where just one of the parameters is unknown. The next example shows how to tackle a problem where both μ and σ are unknown. This will involve simultaneous equations.

Example

The weight of jam put into each jar is modelled by a normal distribution with mean of μ g and standard deviation σ g.

Observations on the content of the jars reveal that 83% contain less than 354.8 g and 8.5% contain less than 343.1 g. Determine μ and σ

Answer

There are two pieces of information, so two sketches:

Fig. 5.21
Contents of jam jars

The 'percentage points' tables do not help in this instance so the normal distribution tables need to be inverted.

z	$\Phi(z)$
0.95	0.8289
0.96	0.8315

The closest the tables get to 83% (or 0.83) is 0.8289. This corresponds to the Z-value of 0.95. So the first piece of information about the jam gives: $\dfrac{354.8 - \mu}{\sigma} = 0.95$

The second piece of information indicates that 343.1 must be less than μ, hence the corresponding Z-value will be negative. The complement to 8.5% is 91.5% so you need to find the z corresponding to 0.915. Inspecting the normal distribution tables yields:

z	$\Phi(z)$
1.37	0.9147
1.38	0.9162

The closest these tables get to 0.915 is 0.9147. The Z-value needed here is going to be negative, hence -1.37. This leads to the equation:

$$\frac{343.1 - \mu}{\sigma} = -1.37$$

or

$$343.1 - \mu = -1.37\sigma$$

Exam tips

Always aim to make this sort of equation linear.

Multiplying by σ produces an easier equation linking μ and σ: $354.8 - \mu = 0.95\sigma$

Exam tips

It is wise to write them out again.

There are now two linear equations in μ and σ:

$$354.8 - \mu = 0.95\sigma$$

$$343.1 - \mu = -1.37\sigma$$

One approach to solving them is to subtract to give:

$$354.8 - 343.1 = 0.95\sigma - 1.37\sigma$$

$$11.7 = 2.32\sigma$$

or

$$\sigma = \frac{11.7}{2.32} = 5.0431 \approx 5.04$$

Therefore, substituting back into one of the two derived equations:

$$354.8 - \mu = 0.95 \times 5.0431 \ldots$$

$$\Rightarrow \quad \mu = 354.8 - 4.7909 \ldots$$

$$= 350.009 \ldots \approx 350.0$$

Stop and think 2

You have been given the answers to questions about finding some probabilities relating to the normally distributed random variable $X \sim N(35, 81)$:

a) P(X < 44)

b) P(X > 53)

c) P(44 < X < 53)

d) P(X > 8)

The answers to the above are 0.1359, 0.8413, 0.9987 and 0.0228 but not necessarily in that order. Can you put the right question with the right answer?

Method notes

Symmetry of Z implies that:
$P(Z < -a)$
$\equiv P(Z > +a)$
$\equiv 1 - P(Z < +a)$
for the standardized values
of $R = 58$ & $G = 47$
  $a = 2$ & 1.5.

Stop and think answers

Answer 1

a) 0.0228

b) 0.0668

Answer 2

a) 0.8413

b) 0.0228

c) 0.1359

d) 0.9987

Method notes

Standardize the various
values: $44 \equiv 1$, $53 \equiv 2$, $8 \equiv -3$
Three pairings can readily
be made.

Questions

1. A student conducts an experiment in the physics laboratory. It consists of suspending different masses from a metal spring. The total length of the stretched spring is measured for each of the suspended masses. The results are recorded in the table:

Mass, x kg	0.05	0.1	0.15	0.2	0.25	0.3	0.4	0.5
Length, y cm	14.3	15.0	15.8	16.0	16.3	17.0	18.0	19.3

(You may use $\Sigma x = 1.95$ $\Sigma y = 131.7$ $\Sigma xy = 33.81$ $\Sigma x^2 = 0.6375$)

   a) Identify the response variable, justifying your choice. (2)

   b) Find the equation of the least squares regression line of y on x in the form $y = a + bx$. (4)

   c) Interpret, in context, your values for a and b. (2)

   d) Use your equation to predict the total length of the spring if a mass of 0.35 kg is suspended. (1)

   e) The student claims that he can use the regression equation to predict the total length when 2 kg is suspended. Is he correct? (1)

2. Two bags contain beads that are identical apart from colour. Bag A has three red and two blue beads. Bag B has four red and three blue beads. A bead is randomly selected from bag A and placed in bag B. A bead is now randomly selected from bag B.

   a) Illustrate this situation in a tree diagram. (3)

   b) Calculate the probability that the bead selected is red. (3)

   c) Given that the selected bead is red, calculate the probability that it came from bag A. (3)

3. A primary school class measured the lengths (to the nearest cm) of 79 pencils. Their results are summarized in the table:

Length (cm)	3–8	9–10	11–12	13	14–15	16–20
Frequency	11	14	24	10	10	10
Midpoint		9.5	11.5	13	14.5	18

The teacher drew a histogram of the data. The 11–12 group was shown by a block of width 4 cm and height 24 cm.

   a) Find the width and height of the block for the 16–20 group. (3)

   b) Estimate the median length of a pencil. (2)

c) Write down the midpoint of the 3–8 group. (1)

d) Estimate the mean and standard deviation of the length of a pencil. (5)

One measure of skewness is given by:

$$\text{Coefficient of skewness} = \frac{3(\text{mean} - \text{median})}{\text{standard deviation}}$$

e) Determine this coefficient and comment on the skewness of the data. (2)

4. The discrete random variable X has probability distribution given by:

x	0	1	2	3
$P(X = x)$	0.25	a	0.45	$2a$

a) Determine the value of a. (2)

b) Find $E(X)$ and $Var(X)$. (3)

c) Write down $Var(12 - 3X)$. (2)

5. Jars of coffee, nominally labelled 200 g, contain X g of coffee when filled by machine. X is known to be normally distributed with mean 201 g and standard deviation 0.4 g.

a) Calculate $P(X < 200)$ (3)

b) Determine the value of the upper quartile, Q_3, and hence find the interquartile range. (5)

A new filling machine is brought into operation. It is observed that 1% of the production weighs less than 200 g. The new machine's details indicate that the weight of the coffee, Y, is normally distributed with mean μ g and standard deviation 0.072 g.

c) Sketch a diagram to show this information and calculate, to 2 decimal places, the value of μ. (5)

d) Basing your decision on the information here, which of the two filling machines would be preferred by the company selling the filled jars of coffee? (3)

6. A gardener planted 25 Tom Thumb tomato plants. She recorded the number of ripe tomatoes produced by each plant. These data are displayed in the stem and leaf diagram.

	1|5 means 15 tomatoes.							
0	6	8	8	9	9			(5)
1	0	0	2	3	5	7	7	8	(8)
2	1	1	3	4	6			(5)
3	0	0	1	6				(4)
4	0	7						(2)
5								(0)
6	8							(1)

a) Determine the median number of tomatoes.   (1)

b) Calculate the upper quartile and lower quartile.   (3)

   An outlier is defined as any item which is more than $1.5 \times$ interquartile range above the upper quartile or more than $1.5 \times$ interquartile range below the lower quartile.

c) Illustrate the data in a box plot indicating clearly any outliers.   (7)

7. There are eight students studying Further Mathematics in year 13 of a school. The students were asked to estimate the proportion of their free time they spent on their Further Mathematics study. These are recorded in the table, as well as the raw mark each gained in their mock examination:

Student	A	B	C	D	E	F	G	H
Proportion of time, x %	12.5	15	20	30	35	40	45	50
Mark y	15	36	33	30	38	45	53	67

$(\Sigma x = 247.5 \quad \Sigma y = 317 \quad \Sigma x^2 = 9031.25 \quad \Sigma y^2 = 14277 \quad \Sigma xy = 11152.5)$

a) Calculate S_{xy}, S_{xx} and S_{yy}.   (4)

b) Determine, to 3 significant figures, the product moment correlation coefficient between x and y.   (3)

c) Provide an interpretation of your coefficient.   (1)

   One of the students asserts that the proportions should have been recorded as decimals. For example, in the table above, $x = 12.5$ should be recorded as 0.125.

d) Explain what difference this change in recording the proportions would make to your answers to b) and c) above.   (2)

Answers

1. a) Length because this depends on the suspended mass (2)

b) $S_{xy} = 33.81 - \dfrac{1.95 \times 131.7}{8} = 1.708125$ (4)

$S_{xx} = 0.6375 - \dfrac{(1.95)^2}{8} = 0.1621875$

$b = \dfrac{1.708125}{0.1621875} = 10.53179\ldots \approx 10.5$

$a = \dfrac{131.7}{8} - \dfrac{1.95}{8} \times 10.53179\ldots \approx 13.9$

$\therefore y = 13.9 + 10.5x.$

c) 'a' (13.9 cm) represents the unstretched length (2)

'b' represents the increase, 10.5 cm, in total length per additional kg of suspended mass.

d) $13.9 + 10.5 \times 0.35 \approx 17.6$cm. (1)

e) The claim is unjustified because 2 kg is outside the range of the given data. (1)

2. a)

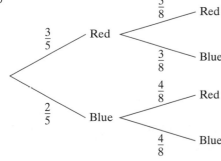

(3)

b) $P(\text{red}) = P(\text{red}_A \text{ and } \text{red}_B) + P(\text{blue}_A \text{ and } \text{red}_B)$ (3)

$= \dfrac{3}{5} \times \dfrac{5}{8} + \dfrac{2}{5} \times \dfrac{4}{8} = \dfrac{23}{40}$

c) $P(\text{red}_A \mid \text{red}) = \dfrac{P(\text{red}_A \text{ and } \text{red}_B)}{P(\text{red})}$ (3)

$= \dfrac{\frac{3}{5} \times \frac{5}{8}}{\frac{23}{40}} = \dfrac{15}{23}$

3. a) 11–12 has true class width of 2 cm, (3)

16–20 has true class width of 5 cm,

Therefore width of block is 10 cm.

Frequency density of 16–20 is $\dfrac{24}{2} = 12$ pencils per cm.

Frequency density of 16–20 is $\dfrac{10}{5} = 2$.

∴ height of block is 4 cm.

b) C.F. of median is 40 (39.5) (2)

Max length	8 ½	10 ½	12 ½
C.F.	11	25	49

∴median $\approx 10.5 + 15(14.5) \times \dfrac{2}{24}$

$\approx 11.75(11.71)$cm.

c) $5\dfrac{1}{2}$ cm (1)

d)

Mid-point, x	5.5	9.5	11.5	13	14.5	18
F	11	14	24	10	10	10

(5)

$\Sigma xf = 924.5$, ∴mean ≈ 11.7

$\Sigma x^2 f = 11\,802.75$, ∴s. d. $= \sqrt{\dfrac{11\,802.75 - \dfrac{924.5^2}{79}}{79}}$

$= 3.52883$

≈ 3.53

e) Coefficient $= \dfrac{3(11.7025\ldots - 11.75)}{3.52883} \approx -0.0404$ (2)

This is very close to zero which suggests the data are symmetrically distributed.

4. a) $\Sigma P(X = x) = 1 \Rightarrow 3a + 0.7 = 1 \Rightarrow a = 0.1$ (2)

b) $E(X) = \Sigma xP(X = x) = 0 \times 0.25 + 1 \times 0.1 + \cdots$ (3)

$= 1.6$

$\text{var}(X) = \Sigma x^2 P(X = x) - 1.6^2$

$= 0^2 \times 0.25 + 1^2 \times 0.1 + \cdots - 1.6^2$

$= 1.14$

c) $\text{var}(12.3X) = (-3)^2 \text{var}(X)$ (2)

$= 10.26$

5. a) $P(X < 200) = P(Z < \dfrac{200 - 201}{0.4})$ (3)

                $= 1 - \Phi(+2.5)$

                $= 1 - 0.9938$

                $= 0.0062$

  b) $P(X < Q_3) = 0.75$ (5)

     $\dfrac{Q_3 - 201}{0.4} = 0.67 \Rightarrow Q_3 \approx 201.3$

     hence $Q_1 \approx 200.7 \Rightarrow \text{IQR} = 0.5(0.6)$

  c)

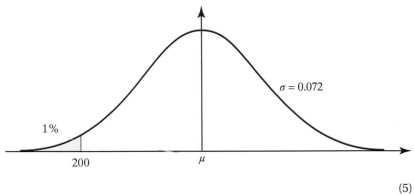

     (5)

     Percentage Points (upper tail) $\Rightarrow z = 2.3263$

     $\therefore$ (lower tail) $\dfrac{200 - \mu}{0.072} = -2.3263$

     $\mu = 200 + 2.3263 \times 0.072$

        ≈ 200.17

  d) The first filling machine because probability of jar containing   (3)
less than the nominal weight is less than for the second machine.
(The second filling machine because on average the company will
use less coffee in filling the jars since the mean is less.)

6. a) Median is the 13th item $\therefore$ 18 (1)

b) Quartiles are $6\frac{1}{2}$th from either extreme $\therefore Q_3 = 30$; $Q_1 = 10$. (3)

c) Outliers are items, x where (7)

$$x < 10 - 1.5(30 - 10) = -20$$

$$x > 30 + 1.5(30 - 10) = 60$$

7. a) $S_{xy} = 11\,152.5 - \dfrac{247.5 \times 317}{8} \approx 1345.3$ (4)

$S_{xx} = 9031.25 - \dfrac{247.5^2}{8} \approx 1374.2$

$S_{yy} = 14\,277 - \dfrac{317^2}{8} \approx 1715.9$

b) $r = \dfrac{S_{xy}}{\sqrt{S_{xx}S_{yy}}} = \dfrac{1345.3125}{\sqrt{1374.21875 \times 1715.875}} \approx 0.876$ (3)

c) Increases in the mark are associated with increases in the proportion of free time spent in study. (1)

d) There would be no difference in either outcome, the correlation coefficient is invariant under linear transform of the variables. (2)

Set notation

$\in$	is an element of
$\notin$	is not an element of
$\{x_1, x_2, \dots\}$	the set with elements $x_1, x_2, \dots$
$\{x: \dots\}$	the set of all x such that …
$n(A)$	the number of elements in set A
$\varnothing$	the empty set
ε	the universal set
A'	the complement of the set A
$\cup$	union
$\cap$	intersection

Miscellaneous symbols

$=$	is equal to
$\neq$	is not equal to
$\equiv$	is identical to or is congruent to
$\approx$	is approximately equal to
$\cong$	is isomorphic to
$\propto$	is proportional to
$<$	is less than
$\leq$	is less than or equal to, is not greater than
$>$	is greater than
$\geq$	is greater than or equal to, is not less than
∞	infinity

Operations

$\displaystyle\sum_{i=1}^{n} a_i$	$a_1 + a_2 + \dots + a_n$

Probability and statistics

$A, B, C,$ etc	events
$A \cup B$	union of the events A and B
$A \cap B$	intersection of the events A and B
$P(A)$	probability of the event A
A'	complement of the event A
$P(A \mid B)$	probability of the event A conditional on the event B
$X, Y, R,$ etc	random variables
$x, y, r,$ etc	values of the random variables $X, Y, R,$ etc

$x_1, x_2, \ldots$	observations
$f_1, f_2, \ldots$	frequencies with which the observations $x_1, x_2, \ldots$ occur
p(x)	probability function $P(X = x)$ of the discrete random variable X
p_1, p_2	probabilities of the values $x_1, x_2, \ldots$ of the discrete random variable X
f(x), g(x)	the value of the probability density function of a continuous random variable X
F(x), G(x)	the value of the (cumulative) distribution function $P(X \leq x)$ of a continuous random variable X
E(X)	expectation of the random variable X
E[g(X)]	expectation of g(X)
Var (X)	variance of the random variable X
$N(\mu, \sigma^2)$	normal distribution with mean μ and variance σ^2
μ	population mean
σ^2	population variance
σ	population standard deviation
$\bar{x}, m$	sample mean
s^2	unbiased estimate of population variance from a sample, $s^2 = \dfrac{1}{n-1}\sum(x_i - \bar{x})^2$
ϕ	probability density function of the standardised normal variable with distribution N(0, 1)
Φ	corresponding cumulative distribution function
ρ	product moment correlation coefficient for a population
r	product moment correlation coefficient for a sample

Formulae you need to remember

Representation and summary of data

For a collection of data $\{x_1, x_2, \ldots, x_n\}$ or $\{x_i\}$.

Mean is $\bar{x} = \dfrac{x_1 + x_2 + \ldots + x_n}{n} = \dfrac{\Sigma x_1}{n}$

Variance is $Var(x) = \dfrac{S_{xx}}{n}$ where $S_{xx} = \sum ((x_i - \bar{x})^2) = \sum x_i^2 - \dfrac{(\Sigma x_i)^2}{n}$.

Standard deviation of $x = \sqrt{Var(x)}$.

Median needs the data to be ordered, then it is the $\dfrac{n + 1}{2}th$ (large n

use $\dfrac{n}{2}th$).

Quartiles are mid-points of lower and upper halves of data excluding the

median (large n use $\dfrac{n}{4}th, \dfrac{3n}{4}th$ respectively).

Skewness: a simple measure is 'mean – median'.

Probability

Events A and B are mutually exclusive when $P(A \cap B) = 0$ or
$P(A \cup B) = P(A) + P(B)$.

Events A and B are statistically independent when:

$P(A \cap B) = P(A)P(B)$ or $P(A|B) = P(A)$ or $P(B|A) = P(B)$.

Discrete random variables

For a discrete random variable, X, taking values, x_i with probabilities,
$P(X = x_i)$.

Probability lies between zero and one, $0 \le P(X = x_i) \le 1$, and the sum of
the probabilities for all possibilities amounts to one, $\displaystyle\sum_{all\ x_i} P(X = x_i) = 1$.

The Cumulative distribution function is $F(x) = P(X \le x) = \displaystyle\sum_{lowest\ x_i}^{x} P(X = x_i)$.

For a linear transformation: $E(aX + b) = a \times E(X)$ and
$Var(aX + b) = a^2 \times Var(X)$.

Normal distribution

For standard normal: $Z \sim N(0,1)$ the Cumulative Distribution Function is

$P(Z \le z) = \Phi(z)$.

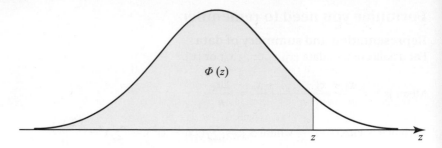

The probability that it takes a value between a and b is:

$P(a < z < b) = \Phi(b) - \Phi(a)$

$P(a \leq z \leq b) = P(a < z < b)$.

The process of standardization transforms $X \sim N(\mu, \sigma^2)$ into the standard

normal $Z = \dfrac{X - \mu}{\sigma} \sim N(0, 1)$.

Percentage Points of Normal Distribution align upper tail probabilities with the corresponding z-value.

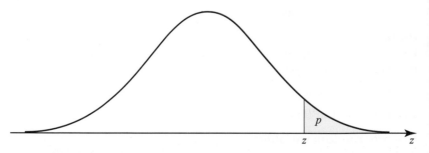

Formulae given in the formulae book

Probability
$P(A \cup B) = P(A) + P(B) - P(A \cap B)$

$P(A \cap B) = P(A)P(B|A)$

$P(A|B) = \dfrac{P(B|A)P(A)}{P(B|A)P(A) + P(B|A')P(A')}$

Correlation and regression
For a set of n pairs of values (x_i, y_i):

$S_{xx} = \Sigma(x_i - \bar{x})^2 = \Sigma x_i^2 - \dfrac{(\Sigma x_i)^2}{n}$

$S_{yy} = \Sigma(y_i - \bar{y})^2 = \Sigma y_i^2 - \dfrac{(\Sigma y_i)^2}{n}$

$$S_{xy} = \sum ((x_i - \bar{x})(y_i - \bar{y})) = \Sigma x_i y_i - \frac{(\Sigma x_i)(\Sigma y_i)}{n}$$

The product moment correlation coefficient is:

$$r = \frac{S_{xy}}{\sqrt{S_{xx}S_{yy}}} = \frac{\sum ((x_i - \bar{x})(y_i - \bar{y}))}{\sqrt{\{\Sigma(x_i - \bar{x})^2\}\{\Sigma(y_i - \bar{y})^2\}}}$$

$$= \frac{\Sigma x_i y_i - \frac{(\Sigma x_i)(\Sigma y_i)}{n}}{\sqrt{\left(\Sigma x_i^2 - \frac{(\Sigma x_i)^2}{n}\right)\left(\Sigma y_i^2 - \frac{(\Sigma y_i)^2}{n}\right)}}$$

The regression coefficient of y on x is $b = \dfrac{S_{xy}}{S_{xx}} = \dfrac{\Sigma(x_i - \bar{x})(y_i - \bar{y})}{\Sigma(x_i - \bar{x})^2}$.

Least squares regression line of y on x is $y = a + bx$, where $a = \bar{y} - b\bar{x}$.

Discrete random variable

Expectation (mean) $= E(X) = \mu = \Sigma x_i P(X = x_i)$.

Variance: $Var(X) = \sigma^2$

$$= \Sigma(x_i - \mu)^2 P(X = x_i)$$

$$= \Sigma x_i^2 P(X = x_i) - \mu^2.$$

For a function $g(X)$: $E(g(X))$

$$= \Sigma g(x_i)P(X = x_i).$$

Normal distribution

Normal: $N(\mu, \sigma^2)$, PDF $= \dfrac{1}{\sigma\sqrt{2\pi}} e^{-\frac{1}{2}\left(\frac{x-\mu}{\sigma}\right)^2}$ mean $= \mu$, variance $= \sigma^2$.

Percentage points of the normal distribution: the values z in the table are those which a random variable $Z \sim N(0, 1)$ exceeds with probability p; that is, $P(Z > z) = 1 - \Phi(z) = p$.

p	z	p	z
0.5	0.0000	0.05	1.6449
0.4	0.2533	0.025	1.9600
0.3	0.5244	0.01	2.3263
0.2	0.8416	0.005	2.5758
0.15	1.0364	0.001	3.0902
0.1	1.2816	0.0005	3.2905

Index

z	$\Phi(z)$	z	$\Phi(z)$	z	$\Phi(z)$	z	$\Phi(z)$	z	$\Phi(z)$
0.00	0.5000	0.50	0.6915	1.00	0.8413	1.50	0.9332	2.00	0.9772
0.01	0.5040	0.51	0.6950	1.01	0.8438	1.51	0.9345	2.02	0.9783
0.02	0.5080	0.52	0.6985	1.02	0.8461	1.52	0.9357	2.04	0.9793
0.03	0.5120	0.53	0.7019	1.03	0.8485	1.53	0.9370	2.06	0.9803
0.04	0.5160	0.54	0.7054	1.04	0.8508	1.54	0.9382	2.08	0.9812
0.05	0.5199	0.55	0.7088	1.05	0.8531	1.55	0.9394	2.10	0.9821
0.06	0.5239	0.56	0.7123	1.06	0.8554	1.56	0.9406	2.12	0.9830
0.07	0.5279	0.57	0.7157	1.07	0.8577	1.57	0.9418	2.14	0.9838
0.08	0.5319	0.58	0.7190	1.08	0.8599	1.58	0.9429	2.16	0.9846
0.09	0.5359	0.59	0.7224	1.09	0.8621	1.59	0.9441	2.18	0.9854
0.10	0.5398	0.60	0.7257	1.10	0.8643	1.60	0.9452	2.20	0.9861
0.11	0.5438	0.61	0.7291	1.11	0.8665	1.61	0.9463	2.22	0.9868
0.12	0.5478	0.62	0.7324	1.12	0.8686	1.62	0.9474	2.24	0.9875
0.13	0.5517	0.63	0.7357	1.13	0.8708	1.63	0.9484	2.26	0.9881
0.14	0.5557	0.64	0.7389	1.14	0.8729	1.64	0.9495	2.28	0.9887
0.15	0.5596	0.65	0.7422	1.15	0.8749	1.65	0.9505	2.30	0.9893
0.16	0.5636	0.66	0.7454	1.16	0.8770	1.66	0.9515	2.32	0.9898
0.17	0.5675	0.67	0.7486	1.17	0.8790	1.67	0.9525	2.34	0.9904
0.18	0.5714	0.68	0.7517	1.18	0.8810	1.68	0.9535	2.36	0.9909
0.19	0.5753	0.69	0.7549	1.19	0.8830	1.69	0.9545	2.38	0.9913
0.20	0.5793	0.70	0.7580	1.20	0.8849	1.70	0.9554	2.40	0.9918
0.21	0.5832	0.71	0.7611	1.21	0.8869	1.71	0.9564	2.42	0.9922
0.22	0.5871	0.72	0.7642	1.22	0.8888	1.72	0.9573	2.44	0.9927
0.23	0.5910	0.73	0.7673	1.23	0.8907	1.73	0.9582	2.46	0.9931
0.24	0.5948	0.74	0.7704	1.24	0.8925	1.74	0.9591	2.48	0.9934
0.25	0.5987	0.75	0.7734	1.25	0.8944	1.75	0.9599	2.50	0.9938
0.26	0.6026	0.76	0.7764	1.26	0.8962	1.76	0.9608	2.55	0.9946
0.27	0.6064	0.77	0.7794	1.27	0.8980	1.77	0.9616	2.60	0.9953
0.28	0.6103	0.78	0.7823	1.28	0.8997	1.78	0.9625	2.65	0.9960
0.29	0.6141	0.79	0.7852	1.29	0.9015	1.79	0.9633	2.70	0.9965
0.30	0.6179	0.80	0.7881	1.30	0.9032	1.80	0.9641	2.75	0.9970
0.31	0.6217	0.81	0.7910	1.31	0.9049	1.81	0.9649	2.80	0.9974
0.32	0.6255	0.82	0.7939	1.32	0.9066	1.82	0.9656	2.85	0.9978
0.33	0.6293	0.83	0.7967	1.33	0.9082	1.83	0.9664	2.90	0.9981
0.34	0.6331	0.84	0.7995	1.34	0.9099	1.84	0.9671	2.95	0.9984

z	$\Phi(z)$	z	$\Phi(z)$	z	$\Phi(z)$	z	$\Phi(z)$	z	$\Phi(z)$
0.35	0.6368	0.85	0.8023	1.35	0.9115	1.85	0.9678	3.00	0.9987
0.36	0.6406	0.86	0.8051	1.36	0.9131	1.86	0.9686	3.05	0.9989
0.37	0.6443	0.87	0.8078	1.37	0.9147	1.87	0.9693	3.10	0.9990
0.38	0.6480	0.88	0.8106	1.38	0.9162	1.88	0.9699	3.15	0.9992
0.39	0.6517	0.89	0.8133	1.39	0.9177	1.89	0.9706	3.20	0.9993
0.40	0.6554	0.90	0.8159	1.40	0.9192	1.90	0.9713	3.25	0.9994
0.41	0.6591	0.91	0.8186	1.41	0.9207	1.91	0.9719	3.30	0.9995
0.42	0.6628	0.92	0.8212	1.42	0.9222	1.92	0.9726	3.35	0.9996
0.43	0.6664	0.93	0.8238	1.43	0.9236	1.93	0.9732	3.40	0.9997
0.44	0.6700	0.94	0.8264	1.44	0.9251	1.94	0.9738	3.50	0.9998
0.45	0.6736	0.95	0.8289	1.45	0.9265	1.95	0.9744	3.60	0.9998
0.46	0.6772	0.96	0.8315	1.46	0.9279	1.96	0.9750	3.70	0.9999
0.47	0.6808	0.97	0.8340	1.47	0.9292	1.97	0.9756	3.80	0.9999
0.48	0.6844	0.98	0.8365	1.48	0.9306	1.98	0.9761	3.90	1.0000
0.49	0.6879	0.99	0.8389	1.49	0.9319	1.99	0.9767	4.00	1.0000
0.50	0.6915	1.00	0.8413	1.50	0.9332	2.00	0.9772		